MAKing
THE
CLIMB

MAKING THE CLIMB

From *SALESPERSON* to *SALES MANAGER* *—and Beyond*

PETER OLIVER

Foreword by DAVID MATTSON

Paperback: 978-1-7351472-4-6

E-book: 978-1-7351472-3-9

To Lisa...
...and to Mom and Dad.

CONTENTS

ACKNOWLEDGMENTS

Without the life's work of David Sandler, the founder of Sandler Training, I never would have written this, so I must thank him first although I never had the pleasure of meeting him. My heartfelt thanks go out to David Mattson, without whom this project never would have existed, and also to the following people who found so many ways to contribute to this project over the two years that I was working on it: Alaina, Brooke, JJ, Ruth, Joe, and Donna (they know who they are); George Donovan, Steve Howell, Jeremy McDowell, Bob Bolak, Penny Sullivan, Roger King, Carol Wolff-Sowers, Tim Campbell, Craig Parrish, Joe Mara, Cody Manning,

Trip Ervin, Liz Duggan, Ryan Soladay, Paul Brown, Megan Bozio, Tim Tormey, Carlos Garrido, Antonio Garrido, Hamish Knox, Troy Elmore, Andy McCreadie, Dan Macias, Jody Williamson, Sean Coyle, Jim Wilcox, Mike Jones, Erik Meier, John Rosso, Mark McGraw, Rochelle Carrington, Rich Isaac, Suzette Patterson, Pauline Cabotage, Drew Rutledge, Lindsay Goetting, Yusuf Toropov, Jerry Dorris, Laura Matthews, Lori Ames, Jena Heffernan, Shannon Haaf Howell, Margaret Stevens Jacks, Désirée Pilachowski, and Jamie Bernier. Last but not least, I must acknowledge the insights and contributions of our awesome clients, who had a huge impact on what ended up in this book.

FOREWORD

The transition from sales contributor to sales leader is one of the most important, and challenging, in all of business. Yet most people who embark on this journey receive little or no training and support in preparation for it. There is a certain "sink or swim" mentality when it comes to identifying and promoting emerging sales leadership talent. And that is a shame.

Pete Oliver's breakthrough book challenges that way of thinking. It is an indispensable resource for any salesperson contemplating the transition into a leadership position, for any leader mentoring such a salesperson, and indeed for anyone interested in developing sales professionals to their fullest and highest potential. Read it, share it, implement its ideas, and spread the word: Becoming the head of finance or the head of research and development or the head of personnel requires preparation, training, and support—and becoming the head of a sales team does, too.

David Mattson
President/CEO, Sandler Training

INTRODUCTION

This is a book for someone making the transition from salesperson to sales leader and for the person managing that salesperson. It offers insights designed to be equally helpful to both, whether they are reading it separately or jointly.

I call the transition to sales leadership "making the climb" because it is a truly daunting journey, akin to scaling a mountain. Planning for and executing this journey is a topic near and dear to my heart. It is one that I have made myself and one that I have helped countless others to make. I know firsthand that this transition can feel like leaping across a chasm with a huge drop beneath you—it is that scary.

Why is it often so scary? It's a result of one of the most common, and risky, decisions in fast-growing organizations—tapping top sales performers on the shoulder and promoting them into leadership roles with little or no preparation or training.

The thinking goes like this: "So-and-so is our best salesperson. Let's make him a leader. Maybe he can get the team to sell like he does." Or: "She is clearly the smartest person on the team, so obviously she should be in charge." Or: "We can't let these two go to the competition, so let's give them those open territories as managers and see what they can do."

The impulses that drive this kind of thinking are understandable. There is definitely an advantage to promoting from within. After all, if you don't, your top performers will likely go elsewhere to continue their career growth. It's true, too, that if someone is transitioned in a way that supports them, the team, and the organization, they can have a huge impact on the success of the business. The question is, how do you successfully promote from within to create truly effective sales leaders? All too often, the transition ends in frustration, stress, disengagement, burnout, and lost opportunities—and I don't just mean revenue opportunities.

Here is the challenge that is easy to overlook. Some of the characteristics that make someone a rock-star contributor as a salesperson can end up being a huge detriment to them as a leader. For instance, the often-praised ability to "think on your feet" and "think outside the box" may show up as praiseworthy creativity and initiative when someone is a contributor, but as a lack of discipline and the inability to define and implement a common sales process once that same person is promoted to management.

This is just one of dozens, probably hundreds, of ways that behaviors that earn approval—and commissions—when someone is selling for a living can show up as a profound mismatch when a "sink or swim" promotion comes along. The consequences of such a promotion are potentially disastrous. If the transition to leader is not properly supported, it can crush the culture of the team—performance will go down, pipelines will suffer, and good people will leave.

Clearly, the stakes are very high.

In this book, I'll take a look at the most common pitfalls emerging sales leaders face, the best ways to avoid them, and the mindsets, key behaviors, and skills needed to achieve success in the role they are preparing themselves for. And, the role is worth preparing for. Why? Because the transition from individual contributor to manager is not only among the toughest you can make, it is also the one that offers the most upside (and downside) in terms of opportunities and challenges.

I wrote this book to help organizations and top-performing sales professionals prepare for, and execute, the transition into a sustainable career as a true sales leader. Too many people stumble into this role and then are expected to stumble upon the keys to success all on their own. That's a lot to ask of anyone. I believe you shouldn't be expected to develop by chance into the next successful sales leader. My aim is to help salespeople emerge on purpose into the next phase of their career—and become true sales leaders.

How It Happened to Me

For many people, the jump to manager is a rude awakening. For me, it was more like a punch in the face.

Early in my career, I was offered the opportunity to manage a technology sales team. I immediately said yes. Why not? I was a goal-driven guy with a relentless work ethic. I had risen up through the sales ranks in my organization very quickly. The promotion seemed like the logical next step. I had overcome all kinds of challenges to get as far I had, as fast as I had. This would be the next challenge, and I would overcome this one, too. I would do what I had always done: figure things out as I went along. How hard could it be?

Suddenly, I was a 28-year-old kid in charge of 16 sales representatives and a $100-million book of business. Only after I had accepted the job did it occur to me that two-thirds of my team was older than I was. This would present a challenge somewhat different than the other challenges I had overcome in my brief career.

Here is a partial list of things I had never done before the first day I showed up for work as a sales manager:

1. Manage anyone.
2. Make a hiring decision.
3. Fire a person or accept a resignation.
4. Give a performance review.
5. Coach a person who had 20 more years of experience than I did.
6. Onboard a person with no experience.
7. Onboard a person with deep experience.
8. Deal with internal management politics.
9. Influence interdepartmental decisions.

10. Create a one-year business plan that impacted anyone other than myself.

11. Manage a profit and loss statement.

12. Mentor an employee having challenges with internal relationships.

13. Deal with any Human Resource issue.

14. Run a team meeting.

15. Interview a candidate.

16. Inspect, evaluate, or offer meaningful feedback about a team's pipeline.

17. Create a template for quarterly or annual business reviews with key clients.

18. Set team goals and make sure they are in alignment with team members' individual goals.

19. Create a new job description.

20. Give a management update to our leadership team.

I could keep going, but you get the idea. From a formal point of view—the point of view, frankly, that would have guided any hiring decision about a critical management role in any other area of that company—I had virtually no experience or qualifications in at least 20 key areas of responsibility.

But since I could consistently execute above quota in my role as an individual contributor, I got the promotion.

Do you see any problems on the horizon?

Once I started to get the lay of the land, I saw those problems ahead, but in response I tried to pretend that I was Superman. *Problems?* I thought. *I eat those for breakfast, and I do it without any help from anyone.* That had been my mindset as a contributor, and I saw no reason to change that outlook now that I'd been promoted to management.

The challenges started rolling in right away.

My third day on the job, I had an employee come into my office very upset, telling me she needed to go on leave because her parents were sick. Not only that, her parents had a gaping hole in the ceiling of their house, and it was raining in their living room. Would I authorize an extended leave of absence? And keep paying her while she was gone?

I had no clue what to do. Was I supposed to empathize with her? Push back? Ask her about the state of her sales pipeline? Ask her to commit to a return date? Let her take a few days off and ask her to check back in when she had a better sense of when she would be able to come back? I had nothing.

Luckily for me, my good-sense instincts kicked in. I had nothing, so I did nothing—until I talked to the resources in my organization who had the answers. Some recently hired sales leaders in situations like this have been known to make snap decisions on the spot, on the theory that not making a decision is a sign of weakness. Those decisions are usually disastrous.

Fortunately, in my case, the people in HR were able to coach me through the appropriate process. But I knew it could have turned out very differently if I hadn't asked for that advice and guidance.

Here I was, a brand-new leader, excited about the opportunity to impact my team's success—and I found myself, in the very first week, having to invest major time, effort, and energy on something that I was utterly unprepared for. As it turned out, there were plenty of management issues that were not only not in the job description but well beyond both my expectations and my experience base. I still had to deal with them. Welcome to management!

I was fortunate. I worked for a great company with a supportive, team-driven culture. I had great mentors who helped keep me on the right path. I had a great team that allowed me to earn their respect while showing me respect in return.

But what if I hadn't had any of those things? What if I had

been missing even one of those things? How could I have possibly climbed the mountain I found myself staring at?

Now, don't get me wrong. I love being a manager. But I need to level with you at this point: I didn't get into management just to manage. I got into management to impact success, to drive the team in the right direction, and to advance my career. I saw the impact that my managers and mentors had had on me, and I wanted to have that same impact on my team.

In the early going, I got a taste of just how much work and learning were going to be necessary for me to achieve that goal—the day-to-day management issues were coming at me hard and fast. I couldn't shake the feeling that I had little or nothing in the way of arrows to pull out of my quiver to fire at them.

I'll make a long story short and tell you now that I made a ton of mistakes along the way. I learned many lessons—some of them painful, some of them expensive, some of them both. In the pages that follow, I'll share the most important of those lessons so that you don't have to make the same mistakes, whether you are the emerging sales leader or the person mentoring that leader.

I'll give you a framework that will prepare you or those you mentor for a smooth transition to leadership success, and I'll share the management behavior plan I have used to guide the behaviors of the salespeople who report to me. (It's based on the behavior plan called the Sandler Cookbook for Success.)

I wrote this book for leaders who believe in promoting from within and for salespeople who want to emerge on purpose as sales leaders in their own right. If you fall into either category, my message to you is simple: Turn the page. Let's get started.

CHAPTER 1

Why New Leaders Fail

I n this chapter, I will share with you three of the most common misconceptions about why sales leaders fail to thrive or to be fulfilled in this position.

Bottom line: Many mentors (and mentees) resist asking the all-important question about the sales leader's role, "Where are things most likely to go wrong?" It's an essential conversation—so essential that I want to begin the main portion of this book with it.

The Superhero Syndrome

Let's start by acknowledging that failure is an integral part of success—a point that is often overlooked by new sales leaders. No one has a clear path to the promised land. There are always pitfalls and roadblocks in the way for anyone aspiring to fulfill their true potential within a given role, especially for someone aspiring to a leadership position. So you need to be very clear about this dynamic up front: You will fail. That is the only path to learning and the only path to mastery. If you imagine you are a superhero or try to act as though that's who you are—the person with all the right answers, all the time—then you will let other people down, you will let yourself down, and you won't learn what you need to learn. Eventually, you'll talk yourself into staying inside your comfort zone out of fear by continuing to repeat what sort of went OK yesterday.

Read this part again: You will fail. That is not up for discussion. However, if that statement makes you uncomfortable, rest assured you're reading the right book. I'll be addressing how to handle failure later on.

The question is, will you learn from the failure and

persevere? The only real failure is if you do nothing or give up trying.

That covers the first and potentially most dangerous misconception, which sounds like this: You are strong and effective as a leader to the degree that you persuade others (or yourself) that you do not or cannot make mistakes.

Holding this dysfunctional belief is one of the major reasons sales leaders fail. In fact, it may be the single biggest reason. This belief is what leads many aspiring sales leaders to micromanage.

In my podcast *Emerge on Purpose*, I interview successful sales leaders. I often ask what was the biggest mistake they made early in their leadership career. Many of them describe a mindset I call "the super salesperson." New leaders, especially those who excelled as sales contributors, often believe themselves invincible and assume they need to rescue everyone and everything. They may feel the need to demonstrate their awesomeness at every turn and prove to everyone in the organization just why they were chosen for this job over other people.

This is the thinking: "Two days ago, I was a peer; now I am the boss, so I had better prove to everyone that I really do belong here." This way of thinking is a serious mistake.

Here's a timeless story:

A new manager gets called into the office of the VP, who doesn't look happy. The VP says, "Sit down. Look, you were a great salesperson, right?"

"Yes," says the new manager, flashing a proud little smile.

"And why was that?" asks the VP.

The new manager shrugs and says, "I give up. Why was that?"

"Because I stayed out of your [stuff]." (Actually, the veep uses another word than "stuff," but you get the idea.)

The new manager's smile slowly fades away.

"Here's the moral of the story," the VP says. "Stay out of your people's [stuff]."

And with that, the new manager left the room, pondering those words of wisdom: "Stay out of your people's stuff."

What did that VP mean? Basically, staying out of people's stuff means to let them drive their own car. Every once in a great while, you might want to point out a shortcut or a cool restaurant they could visit along the way—but don't yank the wheel away from them while they're driving. That's dangerous.

It can create resentment, or, even worse, a culture of learned helplessness. Either will lead to a downward team spiral—and a crash. That's not what you want.

You are not a superhero. You do not have the answer to every question or the solution to every problem. Even if you did, it's not your job to answer every question or solve every problem.

The Control Paradox

The next misconception I'll highlight has to do with something called the Control Paradox. Let's say you own your house, and you also are the mayor of your small town. Will you manage the town the same way you manage your house?

The answer is obviously no. You can't go around mowing everyone's lawn for them. You can't decide to unilaterally destroy the town square and build a shopping mall. You have to work with people if you want to get things done. The point here is simple but surprisingly easy to miss: whenever your world gets bigger, you have less personal control, not more.

Why is this? As your span of responsibility increases, your ability to control things and do things yourself decreases.

You become more reliant on relationships with others, and less reliant on your own ability to complete a task personally. This is the nature of leadership. As a new leader, you need to embrace this dynamic, not fight it. Yes, you need to create the operating principles that will guide the team's success, but you can't go around house to house telling everyone that it's time to pay attention because you're going to show them how to mow the lawn. That is the "here, watch me do it" school of management.

Would you want to work for a boss like that? No, thank you. Happiness in the workplace is directly linked to responsibility. The more responsibility you have for the events in your own life, the happier you can be. How cool would it be if your leadership style promoted responsibility in others, not just yourself? Well, it can—by embracing a less controlling leadership style.

One of the things I love about my business is I get to work with awesome organizations that demonstrate a proven track record of success. But even those organizations can make mistakes. One of the clients I worked with hired a terrible leader to manage their inside sales team. Within months of his arrival, a bunch of their top leaders and sales rock stars had left. Why? Because the new VP had not mastered the paradox of control lesson. He insisted that everything people had been doing before he showed up was wrong; only his way was right. Basically, he either put you in jail or clipped your wings. Why? Because he wanted to make sure everyone knew there was a new sheriff in town, and he thought the best way to go about sending that message was to micromanage everything in sight.

New leaders need to cultivate a trait called intellectual humility. This is simply having the courage not to automatically assume you're right, even when you're pretty sure you are. Intellectual humility allows leaders to see more clearly what isn't working—and more importantly, what is working.

Intellectual humility means being willing to set aside the temptation to prove to others how right you are or to make sure they do exactly what you would do in a given situation. It means being willing to check your ego at the door. You can be a strong leader without having a strong ego. (I'll share some thoughts on creating and sustaining a working culture of intellectual humility in Chapter 7.)

Leadership doesn't equal control and authority. That's a dangerous misconception. Leadership does equal vision, purposeful change, and inspired action.

The Ted Williams Problem

One of the greatest players in the history of major league baseball was the Boston Red Sox slugger Ted Williams—the last man to have a .400 batting average. Yet Williams experienced far less success when he left the playing field and moved into the next phase of his career, as a manager. And his team did steadily worse every year.

Over four years as skipper, Williams won 273 games and lost 364; the team he led, the Texas Rangers, never made the postseason. He was fired in 1972 after the Rangers finished dead last, at which point Williams focused his efforts on fishing—a solitary sport in which he could excel.

Why didn't Ted Williams the manager reach the same heights of achievement as Ted Williams the player? You'll get a lot of different answers from a lot of different people, but the most consistent answer I have been able to track down is that Williams simply had no patience for athletes who were not capable of performing, intuitively, at the level at which he had been able to perform during his playing days. Meaning, basically, he had no respect for anyone who reported to him.

Williams was particularly curt, short-tempered, and dismissive with pitchers, a group he admitted that he had never much liked—not a great place to start if your goal is to set up a strong starting rotation or a great bullpen.

As a one-in-a-million talent, Williams the player had done a lot of things by instinct, things that he often had trouble explaining to others who wanted to benefit from his experience. Another challenge was that he had little empathy for those who were depending on him as a leader. He was not interested in learning about the attitudes, aspirations, and abilities of players who were incapable of competing at his elite level. He believed they could succeed with only minimal coaching and support—as he had done. This was a major misconception and a major mistake.

Like a lot of top-tier athletes who fail to make the transition into management, Williams had no respect for most of the people who reported to him because he believed they were not capable of, or worthy of, being considered his partners. As a result, he treated them as means to an end, not as people with unique gifts, aspirations, and potential.

They noticed.

Sadly, the same thing often happens when high-performing salesperson rock stars are promoted to management. They alienate some or all of their team for the simple reason that the members of the team can tell when they're being disrespected. This is the Ted Williams Problem. It doesn't have to be that way.

Know Where the Potholes Are

If you know where the biggest potholes are ahead of time, it is much easier to steer around them. I have just shared the three biggest potholes emerging sales leaders face. In the chapters that follow, I am going to share tools, ideas, and strategies that are proven to help emerging sales leaders avoid all three: the Superhero Syndrome, the Control Paradox, and the Ted Williams Syndrome.

Chapter Takeaways

- People fail. That's how they learn and grow. If you aren't seeking out failure, you are playing it safe.
- Learn to recognize, and avoid, the Superhero Syndrome, the Control Paradox, and the Ted Willams Problem.

CHAPTER 2

The Success Triangle

P eople, and especially people who sell for a living, sometimes ask me how we managed to get to Maui, where my
family is now fortunate enough to live.

I tell them we usually fly United. Then they smile and say
that's not what they meant. What they want is to know the
"secret" that made it possible for our family to make paradise
(which is the only way to describe Baby Beach in Paia, where
I happen to be typing these words) my home base.

There is no secret. That word implies concealment, and

I make a habit of sharing what I know with aspiring sales leaders. In fact, I'm doing that right now. I'm putting everything I know about becoming a sales leader into the pages of this book, for you. But I think what people are usually asking about when they ask this kind of thing is, "What is the one most important lesson you've learned over the years about sales and sales leadership?" That's a fair question, and it's the question this chapter is dedicated to answering.

The single biggest lesson for me has been learning to leverage the Success Triangle, a simple personal development tool developed by David Sandler. And, by the way, my most successful clients inevitably tell me that it's also the single biggest lesson for them.

What is the Success Triangle? It looks like this:

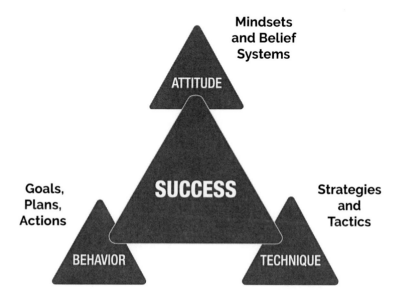

Now, perhaps you're wondering. Why should that triangle matter to aspiring sales leaders—or to anyone in sales? And what do the words *behavior*, *attitude*, and *technique* really mean? Here's a true story that will start to answer those questions.

I've been blessed with a loving wife, Lisa, and two amazing daughters, Bee and Lei-Lei. Years ago, when our daughters were just two and three years of age, we had a little incident that resulted in a nighttime emergency room visit.

The evening started off innocently enough. Just like every night, we went through our bedtime routine with the kids. Now, at this point, I should tell you that my wife is Italian, which means it is basically a moral obligation for her to get each of our daughters' ears pierced at three months old. At least, that's how it is in her family. I was not part of the decision-making process on that one.

So now you know that each of our little girls had pierced ears on the night in question. I have to say they both looked really cute with their earrings on. Anyway, every once in a while Lisa would have to do what we called a "pokey" with the girls to make sure the ear holes didn't close up. Basically that's just putting a sterilized stud through the little hole in the ear. On this night, Lisa was doing pokey with our three-year-old

Lei-Lei, and the two-year-old Bee disappeared into the bathroom. I saw her come back out a minute later with her hand to her ear and a weird look on her face.

When I looked closer, I realized she had tried to put her earring in while we weren't looking. This was a small pearl earring without the backing on it— basically a stainless steel spear with a slippery smooth ball on the end of it.

Can you guess what she did? She put the earring in her ear canal! It was wedged in there, but visible. I started to go into panic mode. Lisa stayed calm and went to get the tweezers. Remember when you played the Operation board game as a kid? Well, the buzzer went off on Lisa. The pearl was slippery, and the tweezers sent the pearl deeper into Bee's ear.

I ran across the street to our neighbor's house, carrying Lei-Lei, the one without a dangerous metal spear wedged in her ear, like a sack of potatoes hurled over my shoulder. The neighbors saw the panic in my eyes as I explained what had happened; they agreed to take care of her. I ran back over to our house as fast as any thirty-something ex-athlete could. Off to the emergency room we went!

Bee was in no pain, but we were worried about her eardrum and that earring obviously needed to come out. After a little bit of time in the waiting room, we took her into an examination room and waited for what seemed like an hour for the doctor to arrive. Finally, the doctor came in, and we told him what had happened. The doctor nodded and said, "I've seen this before."

I thought to myself, *Cool, he's seen this before. No problem.*

"There is one thing I can try," the doctor continued, "but if it doesn't work Bee will have to go to the eye and ear hospital for surgery."

Lisa and I exchanged a worried glance. "What are you going to do?" I asked, nervous.

He held up a cotton swab. "I'm going to take the wooden handle side of this cotton swab and put some superglue on the tip. I'll insert it in her ear. You must hold her still for five seconds to get the glue to bond to the pearl. Then I'll pull it out."

We were impressed. I said, "Wow Doc! I love it! That's some MacGyver-like stuff you got going on. That's going to work!"

I held Bee while Lisa calmed her with soothing words. The nurse applied the superglue and handed it to the doctor. The doctor did his thing—no luck. The swab came out empty. My heart sank. Were we really looking at surgery?

Next attempt. Once again, I held my little girl still. The doctor put the wooden tip into her ear. Out came the pearl!

We all cheered. Bee was laughing and clapping; the nurse handed her a lollipop. No damage done. Her ear was fine.

We got in the car to go home. As Lisa started the car, I was thinking to myself, *OK, what just happened there—other than the fact that we let our two-year-old escape to the bathroom with a little eardrum-piercing weapon in her hand?*

And the Success Triangle popped in my head, like it does pretty much every day of my life for one reason or another.

As Lisa pulled out of the hospital parking lot, I said to her, "Well, that was the Success Triangle in action."

Lisa had heard this kind of thing before. She looked over and said, "Really?"

I said, "Bee nailed the attitude and the behavior, and I'm proud of her for that. She just messed up the technique! We have to work on that with her."

Lisa laughed.

To understand what I was getting at, I am going to have to expand a little bit on that graphic of the Success Triangle that I shared with you earlier. The Success Triangle developed by David Sandler has three points: behavior, attitude, technique. If you want to get better at anything in life, you need to examine the three points of the triangle to establish your current state and identify what you need to work on to get better.

Let's start with attitude. Your attitude can either support your ability to execute and get better at something, or it can hinder that ability.

Let's face it, everyone has head trash: negative self-talk that holds them back from executing on something, and in some cases even from trying. Head trash stymies growth. It may not be possible to eliminate all of your head trash, but that doesn't mean you shouldn't try.

Obviously my daughter didn't have any head trash when it came to putting on earrings. She actually believed she could do it! So when I'm telling this story to groups, I always ask them to give Bee a round of applause for her attitude.

Now that you know what attitude is, let's do a little deeper dive. Attitude is made up of comfort zones, belief systems, and mindsets, both positive and negative. All of these can have a huge impact on what you will or will not execute or accomplish. Clinging to an old comfort zone, holding onto an outdated belief system, or beginning from an unproductive mindset will obviously impact your ability to emerge from sales contributor to sales leader.

You may have heard this saying: 90% of success depends on what happens between your ears. It's true!

At this point in our conversations, the sales managers I work with are usually hungry for some examples, and I suspect you are, too. Here is what a negative attitude sounds like:

- "I'm too young to become a manager."
- "I'm too old to become a manager."
- "There is no way I can hit this jump shot."
- "I can't cook."
- "I'm going to play like crap today."
- "I don't have enough experience to make decisions that affect the team."

Here is what a positive attitude sounds like:

- "I will be the youngest manager in my company's history."
- "I have so much to contribute, based on deep experience."
- "Bottom of the net."
- "I will be a better cook today than I was yesterday."
- "I am shooting my personal best today."
- "I know how to get good advice, and I trust my instincts."

Attitude creates beliefs and judgments. Those beliefs and judgments lead to either effective actions or ineffective actions. But you have the ability to frame your mind to be positive or negative. From the statements above, I think you can see the power of the mind in shaping your actions and ultimately your results. There is a huge difference between thinking (or worse, saying), "I'm going to hit this golf tee shot into the water" and "I'm hitting it in the fairway." (By the way, thinking or saying "I'm not going to hit this tee shot in the water" is no improvement over the first example. You're still visualizing failure.)

Let's look next at the second point of the triangle: behavior. Behavior is the "do it" part of the triangle. What you do is a culmination of your vision and goals, so behavior is all about goals, plans, and actions. What will you actually do? What are the actions you will take in support of your vision? What is your personal *why*, and what goals and behaviors will allow you to fulfill that purpose?

If you don't have your own goals, you'll spend your life helping other people accomplish theirs. Don't get me wrong, I love helping other people accomplish their goals. That's why I got into management and ultimately decided to start my training and consulting business. But that all happened because helping people was consistent with my personal *why*.

My journey, all the way to Maui, has been purposeful. The

behavior part of the triangle is where this purpose comes from. Basically, this part of the triangle is all about asking yourself what you will start doing, stop doing, and continue doing—and why. If you are purposeful about that on a daily, weekly, monthly, yearly, multi-year basis, then you will be part of your own plan.

The baseball Hall of Famer Yogi Berra once said, "If you don't know where you are going, you'll end up someplace else." He may not have realized it, but he was talking about the behavior point of the triangle. This point of the Success Triangle can give you extreme clarity on what your destination will be and how the journey will take shape.

In the case of Bee, our two-year-old, she did a great job with the behavior point. Her decision was do it or don't do it. She did it! I was proud of her for trying. Her issue was not with behavior, but with technique. Which brings us to the third point of the triangle.

Bee's technique obviously left a lot to be desired. She had the attitude and behavior locked in—the technique, not so much. That's OK, though. You can always work on technique. Actually, you can work on anything. That's the whole point. So, what skills did Bee need to develop and improve to be able to put an earring in at a level of excellence? Lisa continues to coach her on that. What skills do high-performing sales-people need to develop and improve in order to lead a sales team at a level of excellence? That is a question you and I will be examining together in the pages that follow.

As sales professionals, as leaders, as people, humans can get better at everything and anything. By the way, getting better doesn't mean just improving skills and techniques. Attitude and behavior are huge.

Let the Success Triangle be your guiding principle for personal and professional success in all areas of your life. That's what it has become for me. The Success Triangle has grown steadily in importance over the years for me. It has become my tool for self-awareness and growth, and it has also become the cornerstone for how I coach my kids, my teams, my clients, and myself.

Years ago, Lisa and I were on vacation together in our favorite destination: Maui, Hawaii. We had placed images about retiring to Maui after our kids went to college on our vision board.* We ended up accelerating our timeline. Here's how that big goal came about.

We were eating dinner at one of our favorite restaurants,

---

* For more on vision boards, see Chapter 12.

Monkey Pod Kitchen, in Wailea. We were sitting at the bar, looking up over the Haleakala Volcano, and talking about the future and our plans to spend more time in Hawaii. Suddenly, our conversation shifted. We started dreaming big—or maybe I should say dreaming bigger! We decided we would move to Hawaii full-time. That vision began to drive our behavior, our attitude, and our technique, in everything we did.

I feel very fortunate that I grew up with two parents, Harv and Linda, who believed in me and encouraged me to dream big. They made me believe in myself. I remember multiple occasions when my dad would say, "Peter, I know you'll find a way to do whatever you want to do. Make it happen." Those words have stuck with me my whole life.

Lisa and I made the decision to move to Maui 12 years earlier than we had planned. We constantly repeated to ourselves: "We will find a way to do what we want to do." And that's what we did.

My dad's words "I know you'll find a way..." connected to every aspect of that decision. He was not telling me how to do it; he was saying he believed in me and my ability to create my own path. These are the same parents who let me drive cross country at 20 years old with my 14-year-old brother. Think about how that decision alone had an impact on what my brother and I thought was possible, along with the confidence it gave us to try new things and explore new possibilities. This is the attitude part of the triangle.

What about the "...to do..." of Dad's counsel? This is the behavior part of the triangle. "Do or do not. There is no try," said Yoda in *The Empire Strikes Back*,[*] one of my dad's favorite films. My dad was coaching me when he echoed Yoda, in the same way my mom was constantly coaching me. When I was growing up and I would complain about something, my mom would always ask me, "What are you going to do about it?" That made me feel like I was in control—which I was. You are, too. The beauty of life is that you can control every minute of every day if you are a part of your own plan.

Dad also included "...whatever you want to do." The key word here is *want*. Success isn't about what you should do— it's what you want to do. I coach people not to be afraid of the word "want." Desire is the connection between attitude and behavior. The word "should" does not support positive behaviors, but the word "want" does. Well, Lisa and I wanted to live in Maui. We made the decision that July day. By December that same year, we moved here.

---

[*]   Also known to the new generation as: *Star Wars: Episode V—The Empire Strikes Back.*

Finally, Dad said, "Make it happen." This last part of his repeated advice is all about taking action. Not just any action, though—action that gets you closer to the goal, closer to Maui, closer to putting on an earring, closer to whatever it is you have chosen as your vision for yourself and those you want to impact in a positive way. This is all about technique. If the skills and techniques you are using do not support the goal or making it happen, upgrade them.

This Moment Is Precious

Lisa and I both believe we only live once; we don't know how long that life will be. We believe life is so precious that it deserves the right behavior, the right attitude, and the right technique, starting now, in this moment. We believe this present moment is precious.

We had some tragedy in our life that made that perfectly clear to us. Lisa's brother died suddenly at 38 while playing recreational hockey. We lived in the same town. Both families had two kids under the age of three. His death was a huge tragedy for our family and still impacts us to this day. When we made the decision to move to Maui, while we never said it out loud, we were both thinking about Lisa's brother and what his loss had taught us.

Chapter Takeaways

- Behavior, attitude, and technique are the three points of the Success Triangle.

- Leverage the Success Triangle to help people determine their current state and their ideal future state.

- Find a way to help people move their lives to the next level, using these words or your own words: "I know you'll find a way to do what you want to do. Make it happen!"

CHAPTER 3

Identity vs. Role and Why It's Important

I dentity/Role Theory, a powerful theory of personal growth and development, deals with two important aspects of personal achievement: identity and role. Understanding and implementing I/R Theory is absolutely essential to meaningful, sustainable success in any walk of life or in any field of leadership. In my view, failure to implement these ideas in some form means failure in life, period.

I realize these are bold statements, but follow me here as I explain the theory. I believe you will come to agree with me by the time we get to the end of this chapter.

To explain the theory, I have to ask you to do a little imagining. Take a moment to imagine that you are in possession of a magical teleportation device. This vehicle can take you anywhere, or any when, that you choose to go. Imagine you are stepping into this vehicle now.

Imagine you are teleporting yourself right now to the safest and most beautiful place on Earth. There is one catch. Before you open the door and step out of the vehicle, I'd like you to leave all the roles you play in life behind. Once you step out of the magical craft, there is only you. There is no role for you to play, nobody for you to satisfy, no expectations for you to live up to.

That means that, as you step out of the craft and into the most beautiful place on Earth, you leave behind your job, your role as someone's child, your role as someone's parent, your role as a cook, spouse, golfer, whatever. You leave *everything* behind. The only thing you can take with you is your own personal identity.

What is that? Basically that's you, minus all your roles, with only your own self-concept and your own self-worth.

So now you are in the most beautiful, safest place on Earth, and you have left all the roles you play behind. Got it?

Now, I'd like you to rank yourself, absent of all your roles, on a scale of 1 to 10. One means you feel terrible about yourself as a person. Ten means you feel great about yourself, absent of all your roles. So where do you land? One? Ten? Somewhere in between? Figure out your number.

OK, let's come back to reality. Full disclosure: the first time I did this exercise, I gave myself an 8. Frankly, I was wrong. Let me explain why.

Everyone, everywhere, is a 10! Literally the only reason anyone would give themselves anything less than a 10 is because they let their roles bleed back into their identity. Think about that for a moment.

Remember, I said to leave all the roles you play in life behind. So why, when I did this, did I give myself an 8? It was because I always have the attitude that I can do better. But— do better at what? At a role!

If you truly are ranking yourself absent of your roles, you would always be an "I"-10. Here's one way to look at it. Whenever you are coaching someone, for example, what you are really coaching is a role. The person is already 10 out of 10 as a person. Whether they are in the right role or have been given the resources, training, and support they need to succeed in a role is another question. As a human being, they are already as OK as OK gets. As their coach, you can help them realize that the roles they play in life don't impact their identity one bit.

Basically, the job is to separate the "I" (identity) from the "R" (role). I cannot overemphasize the importance of this.

All careers inevitably have moments of failure. There will be times when people won't like you or value you. When that happens, it will hurt. But you have to find a way to remind yourself and your people when that happens that you are all "I"-10s. When you do remember that, you can coach the "R."

Coach the "R," not the "I."

The Role of the Coach

Let me pause for a minute and talk about the role of coach, which is often misunderstood.

Coaching someone means you are guiding that person to an improved version of their future self. This is something that happens in private, either one-on-one or in a safe group setting.

A good coach helps you get the most out of you. They don't

necessarily tell you how to do something. They do guide you and support you so you can figure it out for yourself.

There is only one exception to this, and it's an important one: You can't coach someone's "R" if their "I" is weak.

If your "I" is hurting, you will inevitably find a way to self-sabotage your ability to get better. Why? Because your brain won't let your "R" outperform your "I." That's the way human beings are wired.

When you fool yourself into believing that your "I" is less than 10, you say and think stuff like:

- "No way am I that good."
- "I don't think I have it in me. I'm OK being in the middle of the pack."
- "If I beat that target this month, they'll only expect it again next month."

On the other hand, if you get your "I" up to a 10 now, you can be honest with yourself about where you actually are with your roles.

For example, I'd say my ability as a golfer is a 7, using my own personal scale—meaning I am not comparing myself to Tiger Woods in his prime. To me a 7 is the 5-handicap golfer that I am right now. I'm shooting in the 70s most days. Mid to high 70s is now my comfort zone. For me, 80-plus is not good, but low-70s is awesome. But none of that describes my worth as a human being. That's a 10 out of 10.

A few years ago, I entered the 18th hole at 3 under par. Now, I have never shot below par on any course in my life. So this was a special day. I came up to the tee box on the 18th hole. I looked down the fairway. I saw that there was a small pond down the right-hand side and a 20-mph headwind right in my face. What do you think I said to myself at that moment?

Let's be honest, there are any number of things I could have said to myself. Before I learned about I/R Theory, if my identity had been hurting, I might have said to myself:

- "I'm only going to hit it in the water."
- "Don't hit it in the water." (Notice that this is just as damaging as "I'm only going to hit it in the water, because it's sending basically the same instruction to my brain: *Visualize hitting it into the water.*)
- "I will be lucky to come in at one over par. That's the best I've ever done on this course."
- "This wind isn't doing me any favors."

But the truth is, I do know about I/R Theory. I also know about comfort zones, and I knew that I didn't want to find myself stuck in one. So what I said to myself was, "I will hit it in the fairway."

Yes, I understand my self-talk isn't the only contributing factor. I still had to execute the shot. But I wasn't going to let my comfort zone or my attitude get in the way of me performing at the highest possible level.

I'm happy to be able to report that I hit a low fade down the left side of the fairway and ultimately parred the hole and shot 69 for the course as a whole—3 under par.

That was four shots better than my previous personal best. I had created a new normal—in a good way. It feels appropriate to point out here that my self-talk had something to do with that.

What's the lesson here? Simple. Don't let your concept of identity get in the way of achieving new normals within your roles.

You really are an "I"-10. When you self-assess where you are with your roles, don't let your comfort-zone glass ceiling create negative self-talk that keeps you performing at the same level.

At this point you may be wondering, how does this translate to managing your people? Glad you asked. Let me share an example of how I/R Theory applies. Have you or your people ever had a killer month in the role of salesperson? I'm guessing the answer is yes. Let's say you had a great start to the year, and you were at your first-quarter goal halfway through February. Human nature would tell you it's OK to relax and take your foot off the gas a little. You might tell yourself things like:

- "I'm not this good."
- "I can't sustain this."
- "They'll just set my target higher next quarter."

And you'd talk yourself right into a mediocre March.

Why does this happen? The answer is comfort zones or problems with identity. The good news is, it doesn't have to be that way. You can coach yourself and your people to create new normals and expand comfort zones. (We'll look more closely at how to expand comfort zones in Chapter 6.) In fact, as the leader, it is your responsibility to create new normals and expand comfort zones for yourself first—that's called leading by example or leading from the front. It is also your responsibility to begin the vitally important conversation about improving the role performance during private, one-on-one discussions with your salespeople.

Here is an example of how you can position this important conversation with your team members.

- "Are you OK if we carve out some time to look at your role as a prospector? I'd like to get your take on your current state and what your ideal future state is. What would you say is working, and what could improve?"

This is a healthy way to start a conversation to coach the "R." Notice that it assumes the salesperson's "I" is just fine. What's the alternative? Usually, something like this:

- "You aren't cutting it with prospecting. You should be getting more meetings..."

The first conversation starter feels like it will lead to a collaborative look at how the salesperson can improve; the second one feels like an attack, which means the defense walls go up.

We characterize the underlying idea driving that first conversation this way: complimenting the "I" and coaching the "R." Let me be clear. I'm not saying you need to avoid telling your team members the truth on their current state and what could improve. I am saying that you can create extreme clarity around the fact that the conversations revolve around role improvement—as opposed to verbalizing an attack on them personally. When we work with our clients, we start by training the managers and the salespeople on I/R Theory, and we help them get into the habit of using it as a tool, not a weapon. Compliment the "I" and coach the "R."

Chapter Takeaways

- Everyone is an "I"-10.
- Don't let a comfort zone inflict artificial barriers that limit performance.
- Compliment the "I" and coach the "R." Role performance can always improve, but the starting place is always a 10 on the "I" side.

CHAPTER 4

The Behavior Point

The genius of the Success Triangle lies in its three inter-dependent points. Without any one of those points, the triangle would be useless. The behavior point of the triangle, which we will be looking at closely in this chapter, is the "do it" segment of the triangle. It is of particular importance to emerging sales leaders. This point is defined by four things:

1. Your vision and purpose, which create clarity around your personal *why*.

2. Your goals, which crystallize what success will look like for you, both long term and short term.

3. Your plan, which is the bridge detailing out your how-tos. This is the link between goals and action.

4. And last but not least, your action. Your leading behaviors (the behaviors you can count and adjust) are what lead to your lagging results (the outcomes you want to produce in support of your vision, purpose, goals, and plan).

All of what I am sharing falls into the category of, "Do it in your world first, before you try to help someone else do it in theirs." People will respect you more if they know you are walking the talk, and that definitely applies to the behavior point of the Success Triangle.

A moment ago, I made a point of distinguishing leading behaviors from lagging results. This is an important discussion, one that too many managers overlook, because they are fixated on outcomes—typically, closed sales. Closed sales are nice, of course, but just reminding people that they need to generate more of them is not a particularly effective coaching strategy. When coaching salespeople, we always like to talk about the leading behaviors that will result in success. We recommend that every sales professional should know and measure their top money-making behaviors—and no, "closing a deal" does not count as a money-making behavior. It is wonderful when it happens, but it is not a leading indicator of success.

Based on the specifics of a given sales role, the up-front behaviors that correlate with financial success will vary. Here is a short list that is broadly applicable to most sales representatives.

- Asking for introductions and referrals.
- Making LinkedIn connection requests.
- Networking, including via social media (not to be confused with wasting time on Facebook or Twitter—networking is executing purposeful actions that will increase interaction and brand awareness).
- Following up on leads via phone, email, etc.
- Reaching out to closed lost deals in your CRM.
- Making cold calls or, even better, warm calls.

These should all show up in the sales professional's Cookbook for Success—which is what Sandler calls a behavioral plan. If you figure out the right ingredients, determine the right proportions, and follow the recipe, you will get the outcome you want. (We will look at the cookbook in much greater depth in Chapter 12.)

Now, it would seem pretty obvious that a salesperson would need to keep track of this kind of stuff in order to predictably create the financial results they are looking for. It certainly makes sense to focus on these behaviors during coaching discussions. Salespeople need to figure out what they must do every day, every week, every month, and every quarter in order to hit their goals. But for some reason, sales leaders may forget that they need to determine their money-making behaviors, too. Guess what? You do!

So that suggests the questions: What do you want in your management cookbook? What are those money-making behaviors that will make your team more successful? What do you need to make sure you do every day, every week, every month, every quarter? That is something you need to figure out for yourself. Here are some guidelines you may want to keep in mind as you create your management cookbook.

1. **The action must be measurable.** In other words, it has to be an action that can be tracked. We recommend building the cookbook on a foundation of measurable actions with a time-bound element of one week.

2. **You believe those actions will help you and your team achieve success and hit your goals.** The actions inside your management cookbook should support your actions related to coaching each of your salespeople.

3. **The actions should be recorded and tracked on an ongoing basis.** Just as you want your people to monitor the real-world numbers that connect to their leading indicators and ultimately to their revenue generation, you want to monitor yours.

So, what are you measuring on a weekly basis? This will depend on your job description, of course, but here are some likely metrics that the managers we work with have built into their cookbook.

- How many brief weekly check-ins with team members will you hold? These are five- to fifteen-minute sessions where you catch up on what happened last week, get a preview of what's happening this week, and set expectations about any important next steps the salesperson should complete before the next week's check. This brief meeting is not the same as a coaching session, and we recommend you schedule one of these weekly with every salesperson who reports to you, without exception.

- How many client-facing meetings are you taking part in to observe the representative in action? (Note that it is not your job to close the sale.)
- How many pre-meeting planning sessions have you reviewed with your salespeople? (Note: You can download Sandler's famous Pre-Call Planner, which brings consistency to your team's meeting prep, by visiting sandler.com/makingtheclimb.)
- How many one-on-one coaching sessions are you holding this week? (These are extended one-on-one meetings with a given salesperson.)
- How many deal advancement or strategy sessions will you lead?
- How many executive check-in calls will you make?
- How many client quarterly business reviews will you attend?

You get the point. As a leader, you must create an extreme level of accountability and prioritize your money-making behaviors, too. You can't simply expect your team to have cookbooks if you don't track any of your own actions.

This brings us to the next question: How do you create and troubleshoot a truly personalized management cookbook? Here are some ideas.

First off, you probably want to confirm on an ongoing basis that the activities you put in your cookbook actually enhance your teammates' ability to execute. Do the necessary reality checks. It's also important to prioritize the behaviors you think will have the most impact on your team's success. I would also suggest that you ensure a good balance of planning activities, like Pre-Call Planner reviews or post-meeting debriefs, and real-time activities, like client-facing meetings or client/executive outreach.

After you set up your management cookbook, the logical next step is to both do and track the behaviors, week to week. Over time you'll start to home in on the activities that are having the greatest impact on success. Stay consistent, look for trends, and never, ever stop looking for the link between cookbook behaviors and team results.

A good cookbook has consistency. When you have consistency and add the element of time, you can easily determine which actions are having the most impact and adjust accordingly. For example, you may find that pre-meeting planning sessions are having the most impact on meeting results. Or, that role-play sessions have become invaluable with salesperson development. You may decide to tweak your time commitments to create a better result. The reason you need a cookbook to begin with is that time is the only truly limited asset. You want to ensure that you are using the appropriate amount of time to stay proactive in achieving the results you want. Without the cookbook, you'll constantly be in reactive mode. Worse, you'll stay in supervisor mode all the time, never entering into coaching mode. Build your management cookbook to make sure you are doing the proactive behaviors necessary to achieve results.

What are the ingredients in my cookbook? Here are some of them:

1. One-on-one coaching meetings.
2. Pre-meeting planning sessions.
3. Post-call debrief sessions.
4. Attending meetings and calls with salespeople.
5. Role-play sessions.
6. Training sessions.
7. Team coaching sessions.
8. Self-learning time.
9. Time with my mentors.

Notice that each of these is a countable behavior. Here are two sample cookbooks you can use as models, complete with activity targets: one for the leader and one for the salesperson.

SAMPLE MANAGER COOKBOOK	
Activity	**Qty per week**
One-on-one coaching meetings	6
Pre-Call Planners reviewed	12
Discovery meetings attended with salespeople	6
Deal-advancement Team Storm sessions	1
Executive introduction requests	2
Self-development hours	3

SAMPLE SALESPERSON COOKBOOK	
Goal is to get discovery meetings and/or new opportunities.	
Activity	**Qty per week**
Lead follow-up calls	20
Quarterly Value Reviews	1
Asking for referrals or introductions	5
LinkedIn second connection requests	5
LinkedIn other connection requests	5
Networking events or trade shows	1
Virtual or social networking time (hours)	2.5

David Sandler had a powerful saying that allows sales leaders—and everyone else, for that matter—to unlock the immense power of the Success Triangle. Let me share that saying with you as we close this chapter: "Do the behaviors! Do the behaviors! Do the behaviors!"

Chapter Takeaways

- Create your own cookbook.
- Monitor your numbers.
- Do the behaviors!

CHAPTER 5

Your Operating Principles

When you go to a public pool, what do you see hanging somewhere, displayed prominently, so you can't miss it? A sign, of course—one that acquaints you with the rules of the facility. It might look something like this:

No running.
No diving.
No yelling.
No food in the pool.
No fighting.
Parents must monitor their children.

These are the basic operating principles, the most essential "rules of the road" for anyone taking on the role of swimmer in that facility. There's a transaction taking place: "If you choose to play the role of swimmer in this facility, then you agree to abide by these basic guidelines." That makes sense. Sometimes people need a little reminder about what does and doesn't constitute acceptable behavior within the role of swimmer. It's not always obvious to a ten-year-old, for instance, that running on a slippery surface is not a great idea. The sign makes the guidelines clear for everyone.

The rules of the road for someone filling the role of contributor on a sales team are not always obvious and not always simple. Many managers never bother to create or share a written list of operating principles that will lead to the culture and results they want. They need the equivalent of the sign advising swimmers, in a concise fashion, of the rules of the facility.

I've mentioned Yogi Berra's famous insight, "If you don't know where you are going, you'll end up someplace else." But how are you going to get there? What will help you map out the journey and create the culture you want—the culture that will make that journey possible? For that, you need a statement of principles.

Looking back on my early years as a sales leader, I don't think I did a great job of crystallizing operating principles. Our goals? Those were very clear. Our guiding principles? Not so much. I hadn't given the cultural question a lot of thought.

If I'd been pressed to state my team's operating principles, I probably would have said something like:

- "Get it done."
- "Set goals and hit them."
- "Believe in yourself, and do stuff."

Not good enough!

What sign should emerging sales leaders be ready to put up for their sales team? What sign should they observe personally? Better yet, once they step into a leadership role, how can they create a sign with the team's input that will lead to both individual and team success?

Think of this document as your team's sales manifesto. This is a set of operating principles that will lead to success and support a culture that everyone, starting with you, can buy into, support, and defend. This is something you create (ideally) by collaboration through discussions with your team—and then evangelize constantly. Of course, as the leader, you must walk your talk and live by the rules you evangelize.

What could go into such a manifesto? That is up to you! Have some fun with this. Here are some examples of elements that over the years I have helped sales leaders develop to use with their teams :

- "Our personal visions are clear. We crystalize our personal visions and share them with each other."
- "Our goals are measurable. We set our goals yearly and quarterly, and we review them monthly as a team."
- "We make mistakes and learn from them. We love failure because we know it leads to success."
- "We track our money-making behaviors weekly. We know cookbooks are the recipe for success."
- "We embrace both collaboration and competition to rise up together."
- "We are 'I'-10s all the time."
- "We believe in PPPPP: Prior preparation prevents poor performance. (This powerful insight has been credited to former Secretary of State James Baker.) We know that sometimes you need to slow the process down in order to speed it up. We accept that pre-call planning is a must for every sales call on an important opportunity."
- "We strive to be both a mentor and a mentee at all

times. Personal development is a key part of any leadership climb. The higher in the organization you get, the more you need to surround yourself with mentors. Even Warren Buffet has mentors."

▪ "Work hard. Have fun. Repeat."

How cool would it be to go swim at the pool if these rules were hanging up on the wall? Sign me up!

Chapter Takeaways

- Work with your team to create and evangelize a sales manifesto.
- Walk your talk.
- Have fun with this.

CHAPTER 6

The Art of Expanding Comfort Zones

Here's an interesting exercise. Think of the most memorable moments of your life—the moments that really meant something to you. Take a break now and make a mental list of at least one or two those moments right now, before you move on to the next paragraph. I'll wait right here.

Welcome back. Are you thinking of a specific moment or two, or maybe more? Great. Here's my question: How many of those life-changing moments happened as a direct result of you staying inside your comfort zone? Of you relying entirely on what was already familiar to you? Of you avoiding any challenge, any discomfort, any sacrifice, any change in your routine?

Here's my guess: zero.

I've asked people this question countless times. Here are the kinds of answers I've received:

- "The first time I rode a bike without any help from anyone else."
- "The first mixer I went to during my freshman year in college."
- "A 40-foot jump shot I hit to win the game with one second left on the clock."
- "A long bus trip I took with my dad. They lost our luggage, and we had to track it down in Cleveland at two in the morning. It was a crisis, but it brought the two of us together in a way nothing before had."
- "The birth of our first child."
- "The night I proposed to the amazing person who became my spouse."
- "The first talk I gave to a big audience."
- "A huge deal I closed that changed my life forever."

What's the takeaway here? It seems pretty obvious to me! The magic never happens inside the comfort zone. These events are imprinted in a person's memory forever—and none of them are based on staying comfortable.

How can you seek out these moments on purpose? How can you purposely expand your comfort zone and collect more life-changing moments to imprint into your memory forever? That's what this chapter is all about.

One of the big challenges with exiting the comfort zone bubble is that the process of staying comfortable is typically deeply rooted in the creative subconscious. I am talking about a process that is basically the opposite of goal setting. The comfort zone subconsciously guides a person to do exactly what they did yesterday. If tomorrow looked exactly like yesterday, your comfort zone would win. Left to its own devices, it would win every day.

Complacency, the feeling of being happy with what is familiar and comfortable, is a powerful force—a force that can be very difficult to overcome. But there is a counteracting force you can use to loosen its grip.

What acts as kryptonite to the existing borders of a comfort zone? A compelling goal! If you set a goal that excites you, that's a conscious thought. Conscious thought, pointed in the right direction, really can disable complacency. When you set the right goal, you've decided you want to be someplace else or do something else. By the same token, the absence of goals means you're likely to repeat what you did yesterday. Why? Because it's comfortable to do so. That's usually a person's default setting. They roll out of bed and decide they want to be comfortable—that's simply human nature. So in order to get to a place where you are existing outside your comfort zone bubble, you want to set goals that shake up that pattern: goals that inspire you, goals that make you less comfortable with where you are and more comfortable with where you want to be.

Let's look at a proven six-step process on how to expand your comfort zone—on purpose. This is a process I would consider essential for any salesperson, any emerging sales leader, and also anyone coaching or supporting an emerging sales leader. Bottom line: Use it for yourself first. Then share it with the person you are trying to help move up to the next level.

Step 1. Choose a Comfort Zone

Identify something that's currently outside of your comfort zone, something that is a bit of a stretch that you truly want to be, do, or accomplish. It could be anything, as long as the thought of it pushes you beyond a current comfort boundary.

Maybe it's paddleboarding, maybe it's baking the perfect cheesecake, maybe it's giving a speech in front of 500 people. You pick, but remember if you don't consciously decide to take action on it, you will continue to creatively avoid the behavior. The only way for the goal to become real is for you to have a tangible strategy that you want to execute in pursuit of a goal that you've deemed as being both important to accomplish and at least somewhat uncomfortable.

You may have come to the table with a comfort-zone expansion goal that you already want to accomplish; if not, choose something that you avoid doing within your sales process but you know for certain that you need to do more successfully, such as calling high within an organization or upping your prospecting numbers. Identify one such goal right now. Write it down somewhere.

Step 2. Fast Forward to Your Personal *Why*

Let's use the example of calling high-level decision makers within a target organization. You'd never call high in an organization just for the sake of talking to that individual. There is a personal reason why you would want to do that. To find your personal *why*, start asking yourself "let's pretend" questions.

"Let's pretend I actually did call high. What would that mean?"

Here's an example from my own life. I regularly invite sales and business leaders to be interviewed on my podcast to talk about strategies that help people make the transition from salesperson to manager. Early on, I had to decide which guests to invite. The first few people I invited were well-known to me. One was a former business partner of mine who is now a successful chief revenue officer and also a current client. He's an awesome guy and a leader I respect a lot. You know what else? Asking him to be a guest is completely inside my comfort zone.

Then I said to myself, *Self, what if I started inviting people who come from outside my comfort zone?* So I looked at my LinkedIn network. One of the people I saw in there was a woman who was at that time regional president of a huge division of a major multinational corporation. I thought, *That's a good one.* I did know her, slightly, because I had met her when we worked at the same company almost two decades before. But there was no existing social or business relationship any longer. This met my "outside the comfort zone" criterion: It was a bit of a stretch to imagine contacting her. I thought, *You know what? Why not? I'll ask her. It would be a great show.*

Guess what? She said yes. I felt a little awkward calling someone I hadn't spoken to in years, but I decided this was one of those "you miss 100% of the shots you don't take" moments. The *why* was simple: I wanted to create a great podcast and be recognized as one of the authorities in my field. That was what got me to call her. I knew she would know what she was talking about, and I wanted people like that on my show.

Keep analyzing how what you want to do connects to your own *why*. Keep asking, "What positive outcome will happen if I do this?" If you can't find a positive outcome that excites you, keep looking. If you still can't find one, go back to Step 1 and pick another goal.

Step 3. Move from Catastrophizing to Normalizing

When people are about to try anything outside their comfort zone, they often start thinking about the worst-case scenario. Let's say you are coaching a sales professional who is concerned about the perceived negatives of calling high up in the organization. What is that person likely to be thinking?

- "They might be mean to me or try to make me feel insignificant."

- "I will fumble every question they send my way."
- "They are so high up, they'll think I am nothing."
- "They will definitely hang up on me. I probably won't even be able to open my mouth."

Are these really valid concerns? Of course not. But this is what humans do. People go to the worst case scenario because of something that happened to them once or maybe didn't happen at all. Or, they take something that did happen once and give it far more significance than it deserves. Instead, it's better to try to normalize the situation.

Let's examine a scene from a classic movie, *Caddyshack*. In this scene, it was caddy day and the caddies were allowed to use the pool. Somebody dropped a Baby Ruth chocolate candy bar into the pool. All hell broke loose because people didn't think it was a Baby Ruth, obviously.

Everybody screamed and got out of the pool. Management drained the pool and brought in a hazmat team to clean the pool out. Then, Bill Murray in his infinite wisdom, and in full hazmat gear, went over, took a close look and what caused everyone to panic, realized what it really was, picked up the candy bar, and took a bite out of it. This freaked out all the people who ran the club. He shrugged and said, "It's no big deal." The situation went from catastrophic to "It's no big deal." Pro tip: It was never a big deal.

People need to stop asking, "What's the worst that can happen?" It's time to forget that question, or at least ask it in a way that serves you and respects reality. Instead of catastrophizing, ask yourself what the normal situation would be. To me, this is one of the most practical ways of allowing myself to act outside my comfort zone. What is really happening? What usually happens? What is the real-world impact of this new behavior? When I stop thinking about the outliers or the worst-case scenarios and think instead about the normal situation, I can calm down.

Step 4. Isolate Your Strengths and Expand from There

You can find strengths that you have within you to apply to a new situation, even if it lies outside your comfort zone. You wouldn't have survived as an individual without those strengths—humans wouldn't have survived as a species without those strengths.

People have different strengths, some of which they use, others of which they may not. You want to notice your strengths and use them to the fullest. I happen to have a very confident, deep, purposeful tone in my voice. There's probably not a person I could meet that's going to out-voice me. When I need to, I'll use that as my strength, and I'll expand out from there. I'll take some confidence in my tone and I'll use that, even though I'm uncomfortable or uncertain with whatever I'm about to go do.

It's fun to work with someone—let's say, a salesperson—to help them figure this part out for themselves. "You've stated you want to call higher in organizations. That makes sense to me. It will support your goals to sell bigger deals and lock up your clients against the competition. Can you point to a strength that you have that will allow you to do this easier and better?" Stop talking and wait to see what comes back. You don't know what they are going to say, but the important part is that they self-identify something. You can guide the conversation, but they need to own the answers. They might say:

- "My strength is that I'm creative and I keep an open mind. I'll try anything."
- "Well, I have a great network I can leverage."
- "Once I make a commitment in writing, I do whatever it takes to follow through on that commitment. I'll add asking for intros to my cookbook and stick to it."

Help them to find their strength. Then, support them as they work from there. Like a lot of techniques I am sharing with you in this book, this is equally relevant to discussions with salespeople and with emerging sales leaders. Both groups usually need some help with moving beyond their comfort zone in the professional realm. But note that sometimes people are more comfortable starting with a goal that pushes them beyond a comfort-zone barrier they've noticed in the personal realm. There is no wrong place to start with this exercise.

Step 5. Put Your Stamp on It

Every individual has their own style. No one wants to follow someone else's script in life. People want to make things their own.

This presents a fast-forward moment for you as you help others grow into leadership. Encourage them to say to themselves, "Let's pretend I actually did this thing that's outside my comfort zone. How would it sound? How could I make it my own?"

You can do this, too, with your own goals. It's an internal role-play with yourself. You've said to yourself, "OK. Yep, I'm going to do it. I've defined what 'do it' means. I've come up with the normal situation. I know that I'm already good at this one element that will help me. So now, how can I actually execute this tactic or strategy? How can I make it my own?" When you make it your own, it becomes comfortable because you've decided that it's you. You mentally execute the process in your own way before you actually do it, visualizing yourself doing it in your own personal way.

Step 6. Take a Defined Step

This step is where the rubber meets the road. Do something! Nothing happens until you take action. You can get ready to get ready all day long. That's what Steps 1 through 5 will enable you to do. But it's all for nothing if you don't execute Step 6, which is: Do something. Make the call. Ask the question. Get on the paddleboard. Turn on the oven. Take the shot. Whatever the right next step is, define it and do something—and the magic will start to happen.

Whenever you're ready, you can make good things happen—fast—once you follow the process for moving beyond what's comfortable and familiar to you. So can anyone you're coaching.

Chapter Takeaways

- Magic doesn't happen inside the comfort zone.
- Follow the six-step process for expanding beyond your comfort zone.
- Share that process with others.

CHAPTER 7

Create a Culture of Intellectual Humility

When I'm playing the role of trainer or coach with one of my clients, the obvious goal is to help the client get better. Every once in a while, someone I'm working with will say to me at the end of a session, "That was a nice refresher." I once thought that was a nice compliment, but now I see it for what it is: a cultural challenge.

Don't get me wrong, I appreciate the kind words. But

if I peel that comment back, I always find that it carries a deeper, and more troubling, meaning. Is what they are really saying: "Wow, I knew that already but I don't do it. Thanks for reminding me"? Or is it: "Thanks for telling me why I'm already awesome"?

In either case, what they are not saying is what they learned and what they want to change in order to get better. This tells me the person who shares this seemingly innocuous remark about the "refresher" may lack intellectual humility.

All truly great leaders possess intellectual humility. They say what they don't know. They ask people for help. They speak up when they realize they don't have the answer to something important. That's essential if you plan to complete the journey to sales leadership that I call "making the climb." In fact, I've noticed that leaders who don't have intellectual humility tend to *stop* climbing and start camping. Let me explain what I mean by that.

What do campers do? They pitch a tent, and they get comfortable sitting around the campfire talking about the stuff they did or maybe they are going to do.

What do climbers do? They make the climb. They scale the mountain. They push themselves to reach greater heights. They move, they evolve, they collect new experiences. To be a climber, sometimes you have to admit that you need to learn how to climb better. Having intellectual humility makes that possible.

People with intellectual humility have self-awareness about their strengths and weaknesses. They are honest with themselves about what they need to do to climb better, faster, and more effectively. They are also OK with taking wrong turns, falling down, and even failing—as long as they learn something along the way. In short, if you have intellectual humility, it means that you want to learn. In fact, if you have intellectual humility, you will coach yourself and you will want to be coached no matter what your job title happens to be.

As a leader, you want a team that wants to be coached. That's a team made up of people who are the opposite of those who talk about "nice refreshers." After a training or coaching session, you want your people to self-realize what they can do to get better to continue climbing. You don't want people who self-justify by talking about all the things they already knew but maybe forgot or ignored.

There are two types of "experienced" sales professionals. The "nice refreshers" may have one year of experience ten years in a row. The teammates with intellectual humility who have been working for the same period of time actually have ten years of experience because they are lifelong learners.

Combine intellectual humility with ambition and drive, and you have an experienced climber who will keep climbing. That's the experienced salesperson you want on your team.

Here is the point. Having too many nice-refresher-types can kill the culture of your team. They will create a culture of campers, and you as the leader will have a hard time getting them to stamp out the campfire and move up the mountain.

If you are an aspiring sales leader, my challenge to you now is to determine whether your team members have intellectual humility. An easy way to do this is to ask them, tactfully, to self-critique something they did side-by-side with you. It could be a joint sales call, a role play, a planning session—it could be anything. Ask your colleague, "How do you think that went?" The response will tell you a lot. Are they focusing on what they could have improved? Or are they defending themselves?

Three simple questions you can ask yourself and get your team members to ask themselves form the bedrock of a working culture of intellectual humility. They are:

- "What could I have done better?"
- "What will I start doing?"
- "What will I stop doing?"

The point of these powerful questions is to get people to self-assess—not to shoehorn in the answers you feel they should give you. A lot of experts will tell you that when you are giving someone feedback, you should use what's known as the commend, recommend, commend technique: praise, followed by a suggestion, followed by praise. I agree that this is a nice positive way to give constructive feedback, but it's important to recognize that giving feedback is not coaching—it's critiquing.

That's such an important point, and it's so frequently ignored, that I want to repeat it verbatim: Giving feedback is not coaching—it's critiquing.

Coaching is getting team members to self-realize their action steps and then supporting them as they create their own plan to get better. That can't happen without intellectual humility.

You want a working culture built on coaching, a culture that allows for mistakes and failure, a culture where people have the space to be honest with themselves and you about what's working and what isn't. If you make that kind of a culture the daily standard on your team, people will look for ways to get better, not constantly self-justify why they are already good enough.

Chapter Takeaways

- Three simple questions you can ask yourself and get your sales team to ask themselves form the bedrock of a working culture of intellectual humility. They are:

  - "What could I have done better?"
  - "What will I start doing?"
  - "What will I stop doing?"

- Giving feedback is not coaching; it's critiquing.
- Coaching is getting your team to self-realize their action steps and then supporting them as they create their own plan to get better.

CHAPTER 8

Managing Self-Accountability

I personally believe the word *accountability* evokes negative emotions when you say it out loud. I can remember my dad saying to me, "Have some accountability for your own actions, son," in his deep, somber tone. When he said that, it basically meant I'd messed up and I needed to take responsibility for said mess-up. When I hear the word *accountability* that's what comes to mind for me.

Granted, I think having accountability is one of the keys to success. I'm not suggesting that it isn't important. But what does it mean in a business context? Accountability means there are consequences for your actions or inactions. Come to think of it, I believe people respond negatively to the word *consequences*, too. When people think of consequences for their actions, they automatically assume these will be negative. Why don't they conjure up positive images when they think about consequences? That would be a better idea. But, to change the dynamic, let's call them *outcomes* instead. For some reason, outcomes seem positive, but they are basically the same thing as consequences. Cause and effect. Do something, get something.

The words you choose matter. As a new leader, accountability and consequences are tough concepts to master when you are trying to make a connection and build a relationship with a fledgling team. Here is why I'm proposing that you consider changing the language a little bit. Most new leaders tend to weigh in too hard on this concept one way or the other. Either they believe they need to be "the heavy" and show everyone that there is a new, tough, "my way or the highway" sheriff in town, or they want to be everyone's friend, like Michael Scott from the show *The Office*, and they end up struggling with questions like how to gain respect without being a micromanager.

Neither extreme is what you want. You need to strike

a balance. Yes, accountability can always be tied to consequences. But let's rethink this. Let's tie actions to outcomes.

This connection is the key to self-accountability. That is the transformation you are trying to support. When you put the word *self* in front of *accountability*, it becomes much more positive for everyone. It becomes a virtue.

If you track your actions and your outcomes, you will develop self-accountability. What actions will get the desired outcomes you want to achieve? That's a great question for salespeople, and it's an equally great question for sales leaders. Forget about consequences, unless you have the unlikely ability to call sitting on a beach in Maui a consequence. Think about dreams, goals, future achievements. Think about desired outcomes.

If you, as a leader, can guide your team members down a path that leads to their proverbial beach in Maui, then so be it. Bring on the consequences. How do you do that? In David Mattson's book, *The Sandler Rules for Sales Leaders*, there are a couple of rules to live by when it comes to creating and sustaining a culture of self-accountability.

- People work harder for their reasons than for yours.
- See your people through their lens.

To me, both of these rules reinforce a simple concept I call, "The world is not me." That means not pretending that what's important or relevant to you is automatically important or relevant to someone else.

The consequences-led manager says, "If you don't pick up the phone and call some decision makers, you'll be sorry!" The outcomes-driven leader doesn't assume that their own reasons for wanting the calls to happen would even show up on the salesperson's radar. They take the time to understand why each individual salesperson would want to pick up the phone to begin with. This is an extremely important part of the coaching discussion. You can't assume you know what motivates a salesperson. Typically, it is not money itself, but rather something that money makes possible.

In short, consequences imply there's a "should" involved; outcomes imply that they're what someone wanted. This is a key distinction that can lead to the desired changes you want. Find out what they want and why they want it, and lead them to outcomes that make sense to them.

Let's pretend your salespeople could view themselves as a future version of their successful selves. Where would they be? What would they be doing? Why would they be doing it? What is their vision for their life? What do their dreams tell them that they'll be doing? Not to belabor this, but I share it again because the example is apt: I am not sitting in Maui right now because I overcame the "consequences" thrust upon me by some drill sergeant. Lisa and I are in Maui because this was the desired outcome of our actions and hard work—and because we had a shared vision. We made it so because this was our outcome, our positive version of our future selves realized in the present, through discipline and the ability to act with a purpose consistent with our family's vision.

Sure, I'm glad that my dad taught me self-responsibility and taught me to be accountable for my actions. But I'm even happier that he made me believe that I could do and accomplish whatever I wanted. The key word there is *want*.

A vision board—a visual representation of your most important life goals—is an extremely powerful tool for clarifying what you want. If your sales team members don't have clarity around their own personal journeys, help them start that process by sharing your vision board with them and inspiring each one to create one for themselves. (See Chapter 12 for guidance on how to set up a vision board.) If they already have one, earn the privilege of learning what's on it. Find out what's most important to them. If they share it, you will have the opportunity to become a part of their plan. This is the easiest way to manage self-accountability—create a strong link between dreams and actions.

Chapter Takeaways

- Focus on outcomes, not consequences.
- The world is not you.
- The easiest way to manage self-accountability is to create a strong link between dreams and actions.

CHAPTER 9

Develop a Support System

One of the common traits of great leaders is that they are constantly striving to be better. Another is that they never go it alone. Every day is a new beginning of a new climb to a new height. Every day, they are looking for feedback from someone they trust. One of my Sandler buddies, someone I respect a ton and rely on consistently to provide guidance and motivation, once shared this African proverb with me: "If you want to go fast, go alone. If you want to go far, go together." It really rings true.

When I think about the pivotal moments that impacted my career direction, they almost always involved a mentor whose words of wisdom or encouragement changed my view of what was possible. When we were considering the move to Maui, I had a lot of people say things like, "Pete, no sales coaching business has ever been successful in Hawaii," or "Why would you change it up, you already have a great business in Boston?" However, I also had a conversation with one of my mentors.

She and I were sitting in one of my favorite spots outside Boston. She said to me, "Pete, do you believe you'll make it work?" I said yes. It was true—I did. Then she said, "Well, you know what to do then." That's all I needed to hear.

Maybe that doesn't sound like it was that dramatic of a conversation, but it was. Mentors never drive the car; they help you determine where you could possibly go. By the way, we grew the business 80% our first year after moving to Hawaii. I'm glad my mentors believed in me. It made me believe more in myself. On a personal note, I'm lucky that I have Lisa as one of my mentors. She consistently supports our growth and believes in our future. Most of my career-defining moments over the last 12 years happened because we both believed they could happen. That's what mentors do.

Often, you won't expect those career-defining moments to

happen, but they do. Here are some ways to purposely drive more of those moments.

1. **Get a mentor in your company who is two, three, or four levels above where you are.** You'll be surprised how willing they are to help. You'll also be surprised how infrequently they get asked to be a mentor. I've been fortunate in my career to have people like that be very generous with their time and energy. The impacts they will have on you can be profound. More often than not, they'll impact your belief systems and attitudes. Yes, they will help with tactics and strategies, but attitude shifts have the potential to help you see the quantum leaps that could be sitting right in front of you.

2. **Surround yourself with +1's.** There are two types of people in the world, +1's and −1's. Now I'm not saying people are either bad or good. I am saying that some people create a negative energy specific to you and your energy, and others create a positive energy. These are the people who make you feel good, who make you want to be better, for you and for them. They want to become a part of your plan. They want to see your success. They

want to be a guide on your journey. The −1's, not so much. They suck all the energy out of the room.

3. **Pay it forward.** Regardless of where you are in your career, you'll always have an opportunity to be a mentor to someone in your world. Do it, and do it well. It'll create lifelong friendships that will continue to help you both evolve and grow together.

An example about number two above: A few years back we won a very large client. The relationship required all that we had to offer in order to make the partnership thrive. No one is perfect, and that includes us. We had about 12 key members on the team dedicated to this client, but, to speak frankly, there were 11 +1's and a single −1. That one person sucked so much energy from the rest of us that it became exhausting. Did we fix that issue? Yes, we did. The point is, seek out the +1's and make the climb together. It's so much fun when you do. You'll never be able to avoid encounters with −1's, but you can move on and move on fast.

As a leader, make it a point to seek out wisdom and experience. You have to be OK with input from other people. Seek people who can give you advice and guidance without prejudice or ulterior motives. Their success is not necessarily tied to your success, so their advice or actions will not have any selfish agenda.

A long time ago, I managed a growing team in the technology space. A salesperson I'll call Kristina wanted to make a lateral move to come over to our team. The first question I always ask myself when I have a person on my team who wants to make a move is, "Is this the correct move for the teammate?" But that's not what Kristina's manager did. Kristina's manager blocked her from making the move because the move was not in the manager's own self-interest.

The manager even challenged me on that point. He said, "If you were me, you'd do exactly the same thing." I then said, "I absolutely would not. I always support the career path of my people, even if it means they leave."

Imagine the long-term damage this manager did to the team's morale and motivation. They must have been thinking, "Well, I guess I'm stuck on this team unless I leave and go to another company." He created a bunch of hostages.

You can guess what happened next. Kristina left. As leaders, we have a responsibility to play the role of mentor for our own people. Kristina's manager lacked this understanding. Surround yourself with +1's and mentors, but also make sure you continually earn the right to be in that category for your own people.

Chapter Takeaways

- If you want to go fast, go alone. If you want to go far, go together.
- Get a mentor in your company who is two, three, or four levels above where you are.
- Surround yourself with +1's.
- Pay it forward.

CHAPTER 10

How to Not Stink at Interviewing and Hiring

At the beginning of many management careers, most leaders stink at interviewing and hiring. Why? Sometimes it's because they don't yet have an accurate view of what they need. Sometimes it is because they are too eager to make decisions on gut instinct alone. Maybe they have too much confidence that a new person can do the job. Leaders may think, "I did it, so how hard can it be?" Maybe they think they'll be able to get the new person to do it the same way they did it.

All of those are false and potentially costly misconceptions. Hiring the wrong salesperson is the most costly mistake a new sales manager can make. Hiring the wrong person can literally cost the organization millions. Skeptical? Consider these costs:

- The salary and fully burdened compensation.
- The opportunity cost of having a territory underperform.
- The damage underperformance can do to your brand in a territory with clients, partners, and prospects.
- The negative energy underperformance can create for your team.
- The loss of credibility underperformance will have on your management career.

Basically, whatever their on-target earnings are, figure a factor of 25–50 times in either direction to determine upside and downside on the investment. A $100,000 employee is really a $5,000,000 decision—maybe more in some cases. The total downside depends on how long the problem lingers. The upside depends on the fit and longevity of that teammate.

So where can you go wrong? Here's the top four vulnerable spots in the process.

1. You don't know who you are looking for.
2. You don't prepare for the interview.
3. You interview the resume, not the person.
4. You rely too much on gut and intangibles.

Let's start with the ideal candidate. In the sales coaching business, clients sometimes come to us for assistance with interviewing and hiring. We ask all the time, "What type of candidate are you looking for?" Here are some common answers: "I want a go-getter." "I want a hunter." "I want someone who can call high in organizations." "I want someone with a proven track record." "I want someone with a good network." Guess what? Every sales leader wants those things. It's not like anyone's going around saying, "I want someone who sits on their hands, won't prospect, has had sucky results in the past, and is a ghost on LinkedIn." Bottom line, it's time to do a better job of defining who you are looking for.

When you are about to make a financial investment you often hear, "Past performance does not dictate future results." It's the same thing with hiring. There is no doubt that experience is important, but it's not as important as determining the fit. What candidate pool should you be looking at? What is the person's future ability to grow into the role? Will they be able to produce the results you are seeking? These are questions that simply reading an unsolicited resume will not answer for you. You have to dig deeper.

Here are two strategies for dramatically improving your hiring results.

1. Define what success in the role looks like (meaning what are the financial goals and the top 5 to 10 job functions). Job functions are key behaviors like:

   - Territory management.
   - Account management.
   - Prospecting.
   - Discovery and qualification.
   - Presentation skills.
   - Controlling the sales process.
   - Negotiation skills.
   - Networking and partner management.
   - Executive relationships.
   - Strategy development.
   - Forecasting and pipeline management.

2. Use the SEARCH model to determine the "can do" and the "will do" of the candidate within your top 10 functions. SEARCH stands for:

    ▪ Skills

    ▪ Experience

    ▪ Attitudes

    ▪ Results

    ▪ Cognitive skills

    ▪ Habits

Let's leverage SEARCH for the job function "prospecting," as an example.

Skills. What skills are needed to execute effectively with prospecting? Here are some questions you can ask a candidate to get at what you need to know.

▪ **Phone skills vs. email.** "Tell me about how you leveraged the phone as opposed to email to get conversations started?"

▪ **30-second commercial.** "Can you give me an example of your elevator pitch at your last job?" We could do a whole book on this one topic. At a high level, you want to see if their 30-second commercial addresses the problem that their potential clients might have and doesn't simply say how great the product or service is.

- **Overcoming objections.** "The client says, 'We are all set.' How did you attempt to overcome that? What other objections did you get at the beginning of the sales process?"

- **Asking for referrals.** "What was your goal with asking for referrals?" I like to go right to the goal first with this skill. Why? Because most people don't have a goal with this behavior, and they should. I go assumptive with the first question to see if I can catch them giving me a load of bull. I'd rather they told me the truth with this question instead of trying to embellish. It's more important to me that they have good self-awareness and the ability to recognize areas of improvement. After the goal question, I'll then ask the "why" and "how" questions and the truth will come out.

- **Social selling.** "What is your biggest strength with leveraging LinkedIn? Tell me more about that. How did social selling impact your results?" It's good to mix in the results questions throughout the rest of the SEARCH process.

- **Setting meetings.** "What question did you ask at the end of a prospecting call to close for the meeting? What did that sound like? What did you do next? When is the appropriate time to ask for the meeting?"

- **Initial qualification completed.** "What information did you need to obtain to consider the opportunity qualified?"

Experience. The most important part of interviewing for experience is asking experiential questions—open-ended questions about the experiences they've had. Stay away from the "did you"/"do you"/"have you"/"are you" questions—in other words, yes-or-no questions. Questions like, "Do you leverage LinkedIn?" Or, "Have you had success with prospecting for your own meetings?" If you do let a yes-or-no question like this slip out (you'll know immediately because they'll answer yes or no), the next questions must be, "Tell me more about that," or "Give me an example."

A few years back, I was interviewing a candidate for an account executive position at a CAD design software company. I asked her the dreaded yes-or-no "Are you good at qualifying?" She of course said yes. I then needed to switch to an experiential question. "Can you share with me some examples of questions you would ask to qualify a deal?" She answered, "If I can show you how great our product is, will you buy it?" Unfortunately, that is the worst question on the planet—it's definitely not a qualification question. At best, it would set you up to have to pitch too early, but that's about it.

Here are some examples of experiential questions pertaining to prospecting.

- "Tell me about how you prospected in your last role."
- "What activities did you do to generate leads? Can you give me an example of how that sounded?"
- "What process did you go through to get meetings? Can you tell me more about that?"
- "How did you view the prospecting process?"
- "What behaviors led to meetings? Tell me more about that."
- "What were your strengths with prospecting?"
- "How were you successful with prospecting?"
- "How could you have improved?"
- "What did you struggle with? Why?"

Attitudes. This is where you are trying to determine the comfort zones, belief systems, feelings, mindsets, etc., of the candidate. What judgments are they making that will produce results or failures? What head trash could be holding them back? For example, you could ask, "What are your feelings on leads from marketing?" You'll typically hear either a negative or a positive response. "They usually aren't good" is code for "I don't ever call them." The positive response: "I'll take any lead I can get. You never know!" This means they have a positive attitude, and they don't have any head trash about marketing leads. Attitudes are so important because they will impact behavior and obviously results.

Ask questions that include the perspective on their beliefs, thoughts, and feelings.

- "What are your feelings about trade shows?"
- "Can you share your thoughts on our industry?"
- "What do you believe is the best way for you to get discovery meetings?"

Make sure that you have some questions related to attitudes for all of the important job functions that you are hiring for. You are looking for positive or negative mindsets, head trash, self-limiting beliefs, etc.

Results. In addition to asking outcome-based questions during the skills and experience sections, it's also good to leave some time to understand the big picture as it pertains to results.

- "Tell me about your ability to achieve quota."
- "What percentile were you in?"
- "What awards have you won?"
- "What results in other areas of your career would translate well to this role?"

Cognitive skills. Cognitive skills are things like listening skills, problem solving, reasoning, conflict management, change management, etc.

- "Tell me about a big problem you had at your last role. How did you overcome it?"
- "Let's pretend your marketing leads dried up. How would you overcome that?"
- "Can you give me an example of how you impacted change in your last role?"

Listening skills is a fun one to interview for, but I don't recommend that you call it out with a question. Instead, keep track of their ability to actively listen. Are they making good eye contact (even in a Zoom interview)? Are they asking questions and paraphrasing back what they learned? Are they able to summarize the key points that you made about the role?

Habits. During this portion of the interview, you are looking for behaviors or time management patterns that would support success. What do they consistently do that will lead to positive outcomes? Habit and time management questions can go hand in hand.

- "Tell me how you manage your calendar."
- "What does a typical day look like for you?"
- "Do you have any rituals you do on a consistent basis?"

For that last one, I would say, "I wake up every day at 4:00 a.m., and I plan my day out the day before so that I can go to bed with clarity." That's not necessarily the correct answer, but it is a habit that would support success. If you don't have a plan, you'll spend your life helping other people accomplish theirs. If you have a plan, you will have purposeful habits and rituals that will drive your plan.

Are the candidates proactive or reactive? Asking questions about habits, calendaring, and time management will help you determine if they have a plan.

Can Do and Will Do

Your role as a hiring manager is to determine both the "can do" and the "will do" of the candidates. Are they both willing and able? "Can do" is determined by leveraging experiential questions and results from past experience. "Will do" is harder, because it connects to the attitude corner of the Success Triangle—but if you apply the SEARCH model you can crack that code, too.

Chapter Takeaways

- Ask questions within each job function that expand the conversation beyond what's on the resume. This will give you a crystal ball into the candidate's likely future.
- Clarify both the "can do" and the "will do."

CHAPTER 11

Questioning Skills for Leaders

One of the key goals of any leader is to get to the truth of what is happening in a given person's world. (This is, of course, also one of the key goals of a good salesperson.) Truth does not happen without trust. So how do you create trust? I see four paths for this.

- You are (or become) credible.
- You are reliable.

- You create a connection, which means you care and you have authentic empathy.
- You limit self-orientation. It's not about you; it's about your people and your clients.

Now let's take this a level deeper. Basic communication skills will go a long way to assist with building trust in all four of these areas. Perhaps the most important of these skills—when dealing with salespeople, with clients, or with anyone else—is the skill of asking good questions because you truly care about the answers.

You ask good questions because without those questions, self-orientation would be too high and credibility, reliability, and connection would be too low. You ask good questions because if you want to get to the truth, you need to understand your people's version of their truth. It's very rare that the truth is black-and-white. Life is typically a version of gray. And, the correct gray is theirs, not yours.

For example, assume a salesperson comes to you and asks, "What do I need to do to get more meetings?" Or, "How can I get promoted?" Are they asking for validation or because they genuinely don't know? You better hope it's for validation! So let's assume it is. Would you want to know your team

member's version of that truth? If they are asking for validation, it's a smoke screen, meaning it's not the real question
that they wanted to ask. The real question would have been,
"Do you think LinkedIn will help me get new meetings?" Or,
"If I make it chairman's club next year, will that put me on the
short list to get promoted?" But they didn't say that, so you
have to do a little detective work.

A while back, I was hanging out with my young daughter
after a round of golf. We were sitting outside the clubhouse
watching the sun set over the West Maui Mountains. She said,
"Daddy, are we going home soon?" I sensed a smoke screen
question, meaning she was asking for a reason. So I asked her,
"Why, sweetie?" She then said, "Can I have a milkshake before
we go?" Turned out she didn't care when we were leaving as
long as she could get her milkshake first. That was her version
of the truth!

Here is the thing about someone else's truth. You can either
find it out or assume you already know. It is much easier to
know for sure if you ask. You may have played pin the tail on
the donkey as a kid, but, fun as it was, that strategy doesn't
work really well in business or in life. When it comes to your
team members, take the blindfold off.

One of the top questioning techniques of all time is the

reverse, a technique developed by David Sandler. A reverse is answering a question with a question. For instance: "Why, sweetie?" Or: "I'm assuming you must have a reason for asking about [getting more meetings/getting promoted, etc.]. Do you mind if I ask what it is?"

There are so many practical reasons why you'd want to excel at the reverse. The biggest reason? You want to understand the other person's version of the truth. That goes for everyone you come in contact with—and it certainly goes for both clients and the salespeople who report to you.

Early in my sales career, I had a huge deal in my pipeline. I thought I had done a great job qualifying the deal. I knew that the prospect's problem was costing her company over $8 million every year in lost revenue. They had incremental risk that totaled another $80 million. My contact had a significant yearly business objective riding on fixing this problem. I knew their budget and their timeline. I felt like I had it pretty well qualified. But...I lost the deal. Why? I made one major mistake.

At one point in the sales process, the client asked me, "Pete, based on our situation, what solution would you recommend?" Seemed like a pretty harmless question so I answered it. Plus, I wanted to seem like I knew the industry and what I was talking about. I said, "I would consider looking at A, B, or C." Her body slumped in her chair. She told me, "We already tried A and B, and they didn't work." She didn't even want to hear about C. Game over. I lost all credibility right then and there without even realizing it.

What had happened? I basically answered a smoke screen question with my version of gray built in. I could have easily avoided this mistake by leveraging the correct reverse for the situation. Instead of answering right away, I could have said, "Great question. I'm curious what you have tried so far?" Or, "I'm wondering, do you have a short list established yet?" In truth, just about anything would have been better than what I did. Bottom line, I didn't understand my client's situation, and it cost me a commission check that could have paid off my student loans at the time.

That was a very valuable lesson I never forgot. I've told that story hundreds of times in my trainings, and it never becomes less painful. However, failure is a motivator of future success. Experiencing failure and taking personal responsibility for it allow change and growth. Because it was so painful for me, it also became motivating.

Let's apply the concept of the reverse to leadership. Earlier in the book we talked about a common trap that new leaders fall into: playing super salesperson. After reading this far, you now know all the reasons why you don't want to do this. The reverse is a technique that will keep you out of this trap. Assume your salesperson says, "What can I do to turn this opportunity into a three-year deal?" Instead of playing super salesperson and rescuing them, reverse them so they can take ownership of their own path.

Here's what it might sound like: "That's a great question. What strategies do you think might work in this specific situation?"

This kind of question is known as a basic reverse because it reverses the direction of the conversation. It started out with you being put in the position to answer the salesperson's question, and then you reversed that dynamic. The reverse begins with a softening statement, and then you ask a question in return. Why reverse them? Because you don't want to create a culture of learned helplessness. This technique will ensure that you continue to seek to understand their version of the gray.

Chapter Takeaways

- Get to the truth of what is happening in a given salesperson's world.
- Remember, it's very rare that the truth is black-and-white. Life is typically a version of gray. Learn what their gray is.
- Use reverses to avoid creating a culture of learned helplessness.

CHAPTER 12

Vision-Based Execution

For the sales leader and for the salespeople who report to that leader, the best goal-setting process starts with vision and ends with execution. Execution is determined by action; actions must be laid out in a plan that connects them with goals. The plan is the link between your goals and your actions. The plan says what you will do and how you will do it. The goals are why you want to do those things.

In my experience, there are two types of people when it comes to goal setting: journey people and destination people.

Destination people are always driving to the next accomplishment. They see the future. They are visionaries, always striving for what will be, not what is. Journey people are about the process—seizing the day, living in the moment. They are built to be present. They go with the flow.

I don't believe there is a right and wrong between the two styles. I'm also not suggesting that people can't be both. In a perfect world, you want to have balance between knowing what your destination is and enjoying the ride along the way.

You cannot be present without being in the moment. You can't be purposeful without knowing where you are going. When you can find a way to have balance, greater success will follow. For me, this has been the key to personal fulfillment.

I've always been goal-driven. My mind has focused more on the destination than it did the journey. It takes added energy for me to stay present and stop thinking about what's next. I've gotten better at it over the years, but it still takes more energy, conscious thought, and discipline to be fully present in the moment. This was one of the deciding factors on why we moved to Maui. We wanted to live more in the present, meaning we wanted one eye on the present and one eye on the future. It's the same thing when you are leading your people. You have to strike a balance.

Let's take the case of a hypothetical salesperson I'll call Marge.

Marge loves lists. She creates her to-do list every morning. She systematically checks off the boxes. She occasionally does something that wasn't on the list. Then, she'll write it on the list just so she can check it off. The daily plan is clear, but the long-term plan may not be. Then there is Homer. He knows what long-term success means to him. He has no clue what is on his daily task list but is sure he'll find a way to make long-term success happen. Neither person is right or wrong, but both would be more productive if they could strike a balance.

Let me share with you how I do that. I call the process vision-based execution. Another way to look at it is purpose-based action. There are three core principles that drive this process.

- Your reasons are clear (the *why*) and your goals are SMART: specific, measurable, attainable, relevant, and time bound.
- Your path is defined (the *how*).
- Your actions are purposeful (the *what*).

Your Reasons Are Clear

I can't tell you how important clarity is. Why are you going where you are going? Is it your idea? Is it the safe route? Is it the route your parents told you that you are supposed to take? Is it what you were taught in school to do? Is it what's already comfortable? Or, is it something different? Maybe your goal is based on something you see in your dreams—or, even better, something you decide you want to dream about. This is vision. This is purpose. This will become inspiration and give you the energy you need to change.

Personally, I struggled with this concept for years. I was already goal driven. I was very methodical about setting goals, and I believed I could achieve them. My goals obviously changed over the years, which is normal, but sometimes the goal didn't have much juice. I still wanted to accomplish the goal because I said I would, but I really didn't know why I was going after it. Sometimes it became clear that the goal wasn't really all that important to me.

Basically your goal and your vision are two sides of the same coin. Your goal is the *what*, and your vision is the *why*. Your goal is a conscious concept about something you are deciding to achieve or do. On the other hand, when you do a good job creating a personal vision, your actions will start to support that vision even if you aren't consciously thinking about it all the time. The creative subconscious part of your brain has a huge influence on your actions. That's where comfort zones are, too.

If you have clarity of vision, it will help offset your comfort zones and guide you to follow your dreams—instead of mindlessly doing what you did yesterday or sleepwalking through the only life you have, scrolling through social media feeds. In short, it will inspire you to be creative and live life—the purposeful life that is consistent with your dreams and aspirations.

Five Steps to Clarifying Your Vision: The Vision Board

1. Schedule some time to shut your brain off. Go to a place that gives you energy—the ocean, the mountains, a cabin in the woods, a park bench in the city. Turn off all the notifications on your phone. Better yet, turn off your phone period. Go off the grid. The goal here is to get into a focus zone with positive energy all around you. Some people call this type of activity a "retreat," but to me, retreat means "go back." This is not that. This is go forward. Let's call it a "fo-treat"!

2. OK, now that you are in this focus zone with positive energy all around you, it's time to ask yourself the following questions:

   ▪ What drives and motivates you?
   ▪ What/who/where do you love?

- What gives you energy?
- Where do you see yourself in the future (one year from now, five years, ten years, twenty or more years, retirement)?
- What is important to you?
- What do you want for you and your family?

Write down the answers to your questions in a way that's meaningful to you.

3. Pick a canvas, a poster board, a PowerPoint slide, etc. Create a visual representation that is consistent with your answers to the questions above. I like to use a combination of pictures and words that creates a visual representation of my answers to the questions above.

4. If you have a significant other, share your vision with them. I have some clients who create family vision boards that include their family's wants and dreams.

5. Print it out, make it your screen saver, make it your wallpaper on your phone. Put it where you can see it every day.

Now you have a vision! Vision consists of core values and purpose and the envisioned future. This process will play a role in giving you the energy you need to make it happen. It will become your north star, your guiding light. I have a good friend who sold his business in his fifties and is now retired living half the year in Mexico. He says, "I have to be careful what I put on my vision board. If it's there, it will happen." I agree. There is zero chance we'd be in Maui right now if it weren't for this process. The visioning process will take you places that you literally dream of. That is the whole point, actually—to make your dreams your reality. Just a couple days ago, I had a client tell me, "Pete, you are literally living the dream." Amen to that.

Now that your reasons and your vision are clear, let's crystalize some goals that are consistent with your vision. There are three driving forces to setting goals.

1. **You must understand the difference between tangible and intangible goals.** Tangible goals are SMART goals. They are specific, measurable, attainable, relevant, and time bound. Intangible goals are idealistic but hard to measure. For example, I want to be a better dad. That is an awesome goal, obviously, but let's come up with a tangible goal that supports that. Like, I will commit to eating dinner with the family at least five nights a week. Or, I want to be a better husband. Love that goal, too.

How about one date night a week? That's a good tangible goal! It's great to have intangible goals, but you want tangible goals to play a role, too.

2. **You must strive for balance.** Make sure you are identifying different areas of your life that are important to you and have goals in each of those areas. I'd suggest six to eight focus areas. Many people have the tendency to focus too much on one area of their lives and let everything else suffer because of it. Often, health will be what suffers. Creating goals in every area of your life will help you maintain balance. The more balanced you are, the better you'll do in all areas. It's your choice on what your focus areas are, but here are some suggestions:

- Health
- Family
- Personal development
- Work
- Finances
- Retirement
- Fun
- Spiritual practice
- Friends

As a sales leader, you also want your salespeople to achieve their work-related goals. If they have a balanced approach to life, they'll actually perform better at work over time. You can lead by example with this concept. Some people like to live by the motto, "Work hard, play hard." I can respect that. My motto now is more "Discipline equals freedom," which happens to be the title of a great book by American author, podcaster, and retired naval officer Jocko Willink. Both concepts mean you have balance in your life.

3. **You must think long term vs. short term.** Not only do you want balance within your focus areas, you also want balance with long-term and short-term goals. What do you want to accomplish this day, this week, this month, this quarter? What do you want to accomplish this year, next year, in five years, and maybe even longer? Let's pretend you sleepwalked your way through this past week. All you did was react to your day and ultimately be a part of someone else's plan. You did nothing in the week that was consistent with your vision or your goals. You just lost 2% of your year. Let's say you sleepwalked through a year or two. You just lost 2% of your life. That is obviously suboptimal. Don't get me wrong. I really

enjoy helping other people accomplish their goals. I've dedicated my career to that end. But I also want to achieve my own goals and our family's goals.

Your Path Is Defined

Now that your vision and goals are clear, you know what your outcomes will be, and you've decided on your destinations, it's time to create a plan. It could be a business plan, a territory plan, an account plan, a life plan. How will you achieve what you want? What elements will be a part of your journey? What are your opportunities, what are your risks, what are your contingency plans, what are your focus areas? What will you do and how will you do it? This is what goes into your plan. Your plan is the link between your vision/goals and your actions.

Let's put this in the context of a territory plan for a salesperson. Let's say you have a goal of $1 million in sales for your fiscal year. How will you attack the territory to get the most out of your time? How will you guide your actions to create the most success? What are your strengths and weaknesses that will impact results? What are the opportunities and threats that will impact the rewards and the risks?

Sandler has devised a territory management strategy in the Sandler Enterprise Selling process called KARE: Keep,

Attain, Recapture, Expand. If your goal is $1 million, where will that revenue come from? Does it come from:

- **Keeping** your existing accounts?
- **Attaining** net new logo accounts?
- **Recapturing** business that you once had?
- **Expanding** your growth accounts?

Maybe it's a combination of all four. But what combination?

The great thing about a proactive territory plan is you get to decide ahead of time with purposeful planning. Your desired outcome can be achieved easier if you determine where the results will come from and, more importantly, where your time will be spent.

Let's break down an example. Your goal is $1 million. You have $300,000 in existing business, which you will most certainly categorize as Keep. You'll need to determine where the other $700,000 will come from: Attain, Recapture, or Expand? When you think about how you'll prospect within these three buckets, the leading actions you'll take will be very different.

- For Expand accounts, you'll be asking for internal referrals and setting up quarterly value review meetings.

- For Recapture accounts, you'll be reaching out to the client to see what's changed to re-qualify the situation and if there is any reason to re-engage. Perhaps the players have changed, the grass was not greener at that other company, etc.

- Attain accounts, which are sometimes called "new logo" accounts or "greenfield" or "net new," typically require the most time to cultivate but they also can have a huge amount of upside for an organization. Every business is different, but generally, if you don't include Attain accounts in your territory planning process, you will leave money on the table.

I'm writing this book in the middle of a pandemic. Obviously when March 2020 hit, the world changed and everyone felt it. What had worked in 2019 was possibly not going to work in 2020. As an organization, my company had to shift the actions that went into our KARE Territory Planning dramatically.

After you determine where the business will come from, the next step is to determine what actions will drive success in each bucket. That's where the pandemic shutdown changed things for us. Our prospecting, sales, and account management process had to make a huge shift within our KARE model. Prospecting, for example—there were no more in-person client events. No more trade shows. And definitely no more Three Foot Rule opportunities! (If you get within three feet of someone, you find a way to ask them what they do for a living.) For me, Three-Footers happened all the time when I was eating dinner by myself at a restaurant at the bar or on airplanes. Those conversations did result in business for me—but they weren't available in 2020.

So what did we do? We made a commitment to get 100 online/virtual discovery meetings scheduled by the end of Q3. Those meetings could occur in Attain, Expand, or Recapture accounts. We determined which leading behaviors would support the outcome of discovery meetings in those different account types, and we went to work. I'm proud to say the outcome was awesome. We closed more new business during the pandemic than we did in the two years prior. We doubled the size of our team and soon opened up a third location. I firmly believe the commitment to the KARE plan in our cookbook allowed this to happen.

Your Actions Are Purposeful

What follows is a sample discussion that a sales leader (guess who?) had with one of their salespeople. You can have a conversation like the below with every member of your team. Remember, the more you know about the salesperson's vision and goals, the more effective the conversation will be.

"What if I could guarantee, before the year even started, that you will hit your yearly quota? Would you take me up on that? Would you sign up for whatever I'm about to tell you? No, I don't require your firstborn. All I require is your dedication to executing the leading behaviors that will ultimately lead—that's why they are called leading behaviors—to the lagging results you are looking for.

"Sandler calls this your cookbook, your recipe for success. This is the essence of the behavior part of the Success Triangle. This is what you will do, not what you could do. You will do this, which will lead to that, period, end of story. This puts you in complete control of your results. It will also allow you to adjust as the year goes on. Do this, get that. Sounds simple enough, right?

"Let's break this down. On one end of the goal-setting spectrum, you have your vision and your goals. One of those goals is your yearly number. On the other side of the spectrum, you have your actions. Isn't it obvious that you can control your own actions? Those actions will lead to results and outcomes. Some of those will result in positive outcomes and some will be negative. As long as your close percentage isn't zero, you can use this concept to accomplish anything. Imagine dominos falling. It all starts with the first actions, then other things happen.

"For example, you ask for a referral. That referral turns into a meeting. That meeting turns into an opportunity. That opportunity turns into a proposal or quote. That quote turns into a closed deal. The last domino to fall is the deal. It all started because you tipped the first domino over with that proactive referral ask.

"What if you and I figured out how many asks it takes to get one meeting? How many meetings it takes to get an opportunity? How many opportunities it takes to get a proposal? How many proposals it takes to get one deal? If you knew that, how could you not hit your number?

"The only other pieces of data you'd need is average deal size and average sales cycle length. Sounds simple right? It is simple! It's not easy to have the discipline to do those actions every day, every week, every quarter. If it were, everyone would do it. But it's a surefire way to be successful. One hundred percent of the salespeople I've ever coached—including myself—who master this concept, without exception, hit and exceed their number. When I go to my high-performing salespeople at any point during the year and ask them this simple question, 'How many discovery meetings do you need this week?' the answer I get is exact: '2.3' or '3.7.' They know down to the tenth of a decimal what it'll take that week to hit their number by the end of the year.

"It boils down to unique conversations, discovery meetings, and opportunities identified. So, if you can track these behaviors and if you know your conversion rates and your close percentages, you can figure out how many it'll take to hit your goal. I love this concept. Behavior is one-third of the secret to success. The other two-thirds are split between attitude and technique. But behavior can ultimately overcome challenges with attitude and technique. Behavior will go a long way to improving technique and attitude. The more you do the actions and succeed, the better you get at them and the better you will feel about how you're doing. As my nine-year-old likes to say, 'The only way you guarantee failure is if you do nothing.' (Guess who taught her that?) If you are consistent in your behaviors and don't fail 100% of time, you will ultimately always win, guaranteed.

"So here is the step by step process we will use to make this happen.

- Know your revenue goal.
- Know your average deal size.
- Know your average sales cycle.

"By burning this magic success candle from both ends and meeting in the middle, we can determine the discovery meeting number. Let's use this set of data.

- $1,000,000 quota for this year.
- Average deal size of $100,000.
- Sales cycle averages three months.
- Your average close percentage is 25%.
- You turn 50% of initial discovery meetings into opportunities.
- It's April 1.
- You've already closed $500,000.

"So, you have about 25 selling weeks left (half the year). It's April 1, and you have a three-month sales cycle that will eat up all of Q4. So you need to find and close $500,000 worth of deals in 25 weeks. That means closing 5 deals that average $100,000 each. Since your close percentage is 25%, you need 20 opportunities. Since your discovery meetings turn into opportunities 50% of the time, you need 40 discovery meetings in about 25 weeks. And, let's build in some good life balance by factoring in five weeks off over the summer.

"Therefore, you will hit your number if you average 2 discovery meetings per week. Done, end of story! If you hit that weekly target, you can guarantee your results by the end of the year.

"What's the only unanswered question? Isn't it obvious? What do you need to do to get the two discovery meetings per week? That's the magic question. What are the behaviors that you can control that will lead to discovery meetings? How about these?

1. Asking for introductions or referrals.
2. Warm calls: Following up on inbound leads.
3. Cold calls.
4. Follow up on trade show leads.
5. Account management calls to existing accounts.
6. Walk-ins.

7. Three-foot rules opportunities (when we're not social distancing).

8. Email campaigns.

9. LinkedIn 2nd-degree connection requests.

10. Other. I like rounds of golf with people I don't know.

"So now that we know all of that, what should your behavioral plan look like?"

This is the kind of conversation that turns mid-level performers into top-tier performers.

Chapter Takeaways

- Know your envisioned future by creating a vision board.
- Link that vision to your goals, plans, and actions.
- Have a cookbook to take the guesswork out of your success.

CHAPTER 13

Forecasting vs. Opportunity Management

One the key roles to any sales manager job is knowing your business through accurate forecasting and creating predictability. As a sales leader, you learn real fast who sandbags and who blue-skies.

What is a sandbagger? In golf, it's someone that says they shoot 90 but they suddenly shoot 75 (a much better score, for you non-golfers) when the money is on the line. In other contexts, that's called a ringer. Basically, it's someone who does way better than they say they will. It's OK to have one or two of those on your team as a leader because the opposite is much worse.

Blue-skiers, for example, who over-promise but under-deliver on their numbers, are a persistent source of worry. With them, deals are constantly slipping from one quarter to the next. Opportunities shrink in size when the wind blows. Decision makers get a hangnail, and all of the sudden the blue-skier can't get a deal signed. "I can't get ahold of the decision maker." "Let me follow up with them." "I need to touch base with her, but everything should be good." But you know it won't be. For blue-skiers, everything is sunshine and rainbows—until they're not.

At the macro level, if half your team members are sandbaggers and half are blue-skiers, you could get lucky and have a halfway decent forecast.

So get good at forecasting. That's Step 1. Step 2? Evolve into excelling at opportunity management. Forecasting is inspecting the current state. Opportunity management is creating the ideal state by coaching to the gap between current state and ideal state.

Let's start with Step 1. You'd think forecasting would be easy, but it's definitely not. It doesn't just happen. A sizeable portion of salespeople who are skilled at other things are not very good at forecasting, and wrong forecasts can make you look bad as a leader. Nothing will get a sales leader in hot water quicker with higher ups than frequently missing forecasts. After messing up a forecast call once or twice, it's tempting to start micromanaging a pipeline—basically, calling a salesperson out on anything that isn't solid. At best, leaders will micromanage. At worst, they can turn into the critical parent who makes the team member want to rebel. The leader will say, "Why didn't you validate their timeline and know their purchase order process?" The salesperson will say, "Well, if our product were better, they would have already bought it." Kind of like when you say to your kids, "Eat your veggies." Then, they go draw on the walls with a Sharpie. That's always fun, for both sides.

Seriously though, how do you get accurate forecasts without turning into a micromanager or a critical parent? At the very least, make sure your sales process is extremely clear. What are the steps, phases, or gates? What is required to forecast a low, most likely, and best case? What is required to commit a deal to your forecast? How do the salespeople validate the unknowns with the client? What does "qualified" actually mean? If all this is extremely clear and the expectations are set, all you'd need to do is manage the deltas. Sandler's process for managing deals is extremely simple and logical. Why? Because it follows a clear sales process.

Nothing goes into motion unless the prospect or client has decided they have a gap between where they are and where they want to be. We call that gap "pain." To expand on that, there are two buying emotions: pain and pleasure. People and companies will decide to change if 1) they have pain now or believe they may have pain in the future or 2) they are seeking out instant gratification around pleasure or they want pleasure in the future. Without this, do not pass go, do not collect $200. This is the most important part of any forecast, period—a clear understanding of the client's pain.

Some other forecasting methodologies out there have catchy acronyms like BANT (budget, authority, need, timeline). These can be good lists of elements you should know to forecast a deal, but they sometimes create bad habits because they are often in the wrong order. How do you coach someone to use the BANT acronym? It's not like you can walk up to a client and say, "Hey, nice to meet you—what's your budget?"

Bottom line, your forecast methodology should match

your sales process. Your sales process should match the buying process of your clients. A frictionless sales process should mirror the ideal buying process. An accurate forecast methodology should predict results based on your ability to map your sales process to the prospect's buying process. It's not enough to have a checklist of qualification items—it has to be done in the right order.

The buying process absolutely starts with pain. Without it, nothing else really matters. If you don't define pain, every other qualification item like budget and timelines are worthless. You want to elevate your forecast methodology? Here are three tips: pain, pain, pain. Why? Pain is the genesis of all decisions.

These are the questions organizations are asking themselves:

1. "Does my organization have a problem?"
2. "How much is the problem costing my organization in terms of money, risk, resources, time, etc.?"
3. "How is the problem impacting me personally?"
4. "How does this problem stack up against all our other priorities?"
5. "Is it worth changing, or can we live with it?"

The company decision makers will not move forward on a purchase without clear answers to these five questions.

Now, let's be real. There are plenty of times when a salesperson gets the deal without knowing the answer to these five questions. But just because they didn't find out doesn't mean the answers weren't there to be found. That salesperson just got lucky. Organizations will sometimes buy in spite of the salesperson, not because of them. Why? Because they already answered the five questions above and decided it was worth changing. So why are some forecasts riddled with problems? The biggest reason is that they find out the answer to Question 1 and forget about Questions 2, 3, 4, and 5 until it's too late.

The client might say, "Do you have products or services that can help give me more visibility?" The salesperson thinks, *Wow! I have a live one! Let's yank this fish in the boat before it gets away!* What do they start doing? Selling of course. They will sell on the *what* instead of getting to the *why*. Then equally important, they do not validate the importance and commitment to the *why*.

The salesperson will present too early, then go back and try to fill in the gaps with the forecast. After the fact, they start chasing questions because their forecast acronyms have gaps in timeline, decision-making process, budget, etc. It's pretty likely the company already had their timelines established and their decision criteria and process defined, but the salesperson never found out the truth. Why? They didn't qualify. Bad qualification means bad forecasts.

Let me attempt to simplify a process that will result in accurate forecasts.

First, find the pain.

- What's the problem?
- How is it impacting the company? Try to put a dollar amount on the problem.
- Let's pretend they do nothing. What does it mean in terms of dollars if the problem doesn't get fixed?
- How is it impacting the person you are talking to?
- What is the relative importance of this impact compared to everything else they are dealing with?
- Is status quo an option, or have they decided they need to change?

Second, qualify everything like you have a time machine sitting in your driveway. Find out what will happen and how it will happen before it actually happens.

Ask them: "Let's pretend you believe there is a fit. Is there a date you are targeting to have a solution in place?

Let's fast forward a little. Assuming you decide you want to move forward in the process, who in addition to yourself will be involved?"

The beauty of asking questions like this early in the sales process is that it's in the best interest of yourself and the client. If you don't know the answers to these questions, then you can't support their buying process. Ineffective salespeople will end up blaming the clients for their own poor forecasts. "They didn't have enough money." Really? Maybe you didn't find out what their budget cycle actually looked like. Maybe you were dealing with someone who had no clue how they could go find the money.

David Sandler used to say, "There are no bad prospects, only bad salespeople."

In addition to pain, what else would mean you have a qualified deal? This a question that you need to decide as a leader. Typically there are two categories of qualification.

Business Qualification

- Problem
- Reason for the problem
- Why they care
- What they've tried/current solution

- Financial impact
- Desired outcomes
- Personal reason
- Committed to change/project defined
- Relative importance compared to other projects
- Budget
- Willingness to commit time and resources
- Budget approval process
- Timeline and milestones
- The *why* behind the timeline and milestones
- Decision process defined
- Decision criteria and success factors defined
- All decision makers identified
- Clear procurement process (contract signed, now what?)
- Clear implementation plan
- Verbal yes from coach or sponsor
- Champion validated
- Partner engaged (if applicable)

Situational or Technical Qualification

- Does this situation fit your ideal client profile?
- Is it big enough/small enough?

- Do they have the right environment for your solution to work?
- Are they locked into an agreement they can't get out of?

These items tend to be industry specific, but it's important not to waste time on someone who was never going to buy. After all, the only truly limited asset is time.

OK, you now have a forecast that is accurate and rooted in the truth because your sales process matches the clients' buying process. Your sales team has re-ordered their qualification acronyms to map to pain first and everything else second.

Here are three simple rules that will help you dictate the order of your qualification process.

Rule 1. Pain first. I think we've covered this in sufficient depth for you to understand just how important it is.

Rule 2. Don't talk about money unless they are emotional about their own pain. Without pain, all you have is price. The more pain you have, the less price matters. In order to have a productive conversation about money, it helps if you have that dialog on the heels of the pain conversation.

Rule 3. Don't assume anything regarding their decision-making process.

- When are they making the decision?

- Why is that the date?
- How will they decide?
- What is the success criteria?
- What is the process?
- Who will play a role in the process?

One of my clients, who sold airplane parts, was going through a proof of concept phase with an airplane manufacturer. My client assumed that if the trial went well, the manufacturer would place an order for the $5 million worth of parts. The trial ended, and the supplier passed with flying colors. The manufacturer loved the solution, and it fit with what they needed. My client then asked for the order because they assumed the timeline made sense. At which point, their prospect said, "Oh no, we are pre-planning our production process for a plane we will start to manufacture two years from now." Wait, what?!

That deal was 90% in the forecast for that quarter. What happened? The obvious issue was that the salesperson got excited and started selling without truly qualifying. In this case, they didn't ask about the purchasing timeline, which was different from the decision-making timeline.

Stories like this are endless and riddled throughout poor forecasts. I'm sure most sales leaders could write huge books on all the deals they didn't get. But what if you solved this forecasting problem, perhaps because your sales professionals become heat-seeking, pain-finding missiles and continue their qualification process until they have every prospect fully qualified? What's next?

Congratulations! Now you are a sales leader with an accurate forecast. You get to keep your job for a while.

Opportunity Management

Let's talk about opportunity management. Having an accurate forecast means you are on your way to becoming a good supervisor. Supervision, though, is about the current state. What you want is to be coaching to the future state. To say it another way, forecasting is inspecting, or scrubbing, or validating the current state of the pipeline. Opportunity management is impacting the future output of the pipeline.

Here is an acronym I actually love—not only because in my twenties I had a cigar locker at the Punch Bar in the Sheraton Hotel in Boston, but also because it works.

CIGAR

- Current state
- Ideal state

- Gap
- Action
- Recap

The majority of forecast calls begin and end with validating the current state. If you want to evolve from being a supervisor to being a coach, you want to evolve the conversation beyond the "C" to include the "I" and the "G." Managing the opportunity means you are constantly looking for ways to achieve the ideal state in every deal within the stages or steps that your organization follows. In order to move from stage to stage, you must accomplish certain elements. For example, you should require a clear understanding of the client's pain, budget process, and decision-making process in order for the deal to be considered qualified.

Part of understanding the decision-making process is understanding who all the players are. Let's pretend you are dealing with someone who needs to go one level up for a signature. This deal probably should not be considered a high probability unless that selling challenge is overcome. What will the supervisor do? They'll try to identify the exaggerations. Ask, "Are you dealing with authority or the economic buyer?" "Did you validate the champion?" Use lots of yes/no closed-ended questions to check the box on everything that would be needed given the stage or forecast level of the deal. Again, you are validating the "C" in CIGAR.

But let's follow the progression forward. How do you make the ideal state of the deal happen? Find out not only where you are but where you want to be with this deal. For example, if you haven't involved the appropriate levels in the organization, then you should do that next. The big question is how. That's what a coach does—inspires creative conversions from current to ideal state. Any question related to how means it will be open-ended.

Let's examine how to involve the appropriate people in the organization. This will make the gap very clear. As coaches, start asking questions like, "How can we earn the right to get an audience with the CEO?" "How will this solution create the business outcomes that this type of decision maker will care about?" "How do we validate that the people we are dealing with are willing to go to bat for your solution, or are they still on the fence?" Bottom line, you want to come up with a plan to involve all the decision makers. After that? It is on to action steps and recap. CIGAR!

Let's put the CIGAR method into the concept of time. Let's say you are having a one-on-one with a team member for an hour and you want to work on opportunity management, not just forecasting. In that hour, 10% of the time should be spent on the current state, 70% on the ideal state and the gap, and 20% on action and recap.

Have you ever been to the Stage Deli in New York City? Their corned beef Reuben sandwich is what you want your opportunity management sessions to be like. The supervisor is the rye bread. The bread has a purpose; even though it's a little bitter, it keeps the corned beef in place. It is necessary for the sandwich to exist. The corned beef, sauerkraut, Russian dressing, and Swiss is the coach. That is where all the flavor and substance are. The better the coach, the bigger the sandwich.

Master opportunity management and you'll be the Stage Deli Reuben of the sales management ranks. That's saying something! Nobody wants a manager who is simply two pieces of bitter bread. Use CIGAR to make some kickass sandwiches with your team with lots of meat in the middle. The meat is the coaching. Fill it up even if it takes multiple helpings to eat it all. Better yet, let your sales professionals determine what type of ingredients go into the coaching discussions. If they own their own coaching plan, the results will improve because they are accountable to their own journey.

Chapter Takeaways

- Having a couple of sandbaggers on your team is not a problem. Having even one blue-skier is a problem. Help blue-skiers create more realistic estimates.

- To do this, make sure your sales process is extremely clear. What are the steps, phases, or gates? What is required to forecast a low, most likely, and best case? What is required to commit to a deal? What does "qualified" actually mean? All this must be extremely clear, and the right expectations must be set.

- Forecasting is inspecting, scrubbing, and validating the current state of the pipeline. Opportunity management is impacting the future output of the pipeline.

CHAPTER 14

How to Listen

Years ago when I had my first management job running a sales region in New England, our company president flew up from Texas to visit some clients with me. If you have ever spent any time in Massachusetts, you know that traffic around Boston is terrible. We had a lot of windshield time together as we went from client to client.

I remember vividly driving around from Bose in Framingham to State Street Bank in Quincy. We were driving down Interstate 93 having a conversation about my team. The company president asked me all kinds of questions about my team's structure and what I thought needed to change. He was four levels above me in the organization, but he actually acted like he cared about my ideas and opinions. That was because he actually did.

Six months later at our sales kick-off, he announced that our company was changing our coverage model for our mid-market business. After his keynote, I went up to him to thank him for making some of the changes I'd suggested. I was really excited about it. He said, "Pete, do you remember that conversation we had while I was in Boston visiting clients with you?" I replied, "Of course." He said, "I listened." I never forgot that.

Obviously I was glad I played a small part in our company's go-to-market strategy. I was more excited that I worked for a company with a president who listened to his people. He was running a $2 billion business but made time to listen. Ironically, the go-to-market strategy decisions that he made opened up headcounts, one of which would later be filled by my future wife, Lisa. When leaders listen, cool things happen.

Recently my client Regina shared a story about this. She was executing a vision board exercise with her team. Multiple people thanked her afterwards. They really appreciated that Regina cared enough to ask them what was important to them. They felt supported in their journey. Why? Because she listened, which authentically showed that she cared.

Early in my management career I struggled with this concept. I'll admit it. I had a couple team members who would call me out on it. They'd come in my office, and we'd start to have a conversation. At some point, I'd lose interest and start looking down at my computer. It immediately gave them the feeling that I didn't care what they were saying. Maybe sometimes that was true and maybe other times I did care but I was trying to multitask, but it was always a turnoff. Now, it's obvious to me; then, it wasn't. Whether I cared or not, they assumed I didn't because they could tell I wasn't actively listening.

Bottom line, be present. Turn off phone notifications when you have meetings or one-on-ones. Don't have multiple screens open. Stop scrolling when you should be listening.

One of the main areas where salespeople feel unlistened to and, let's be honest, disrespected, is during team meetings. Here are seven vitally important rules for sales leaders on running an effective team meeting where team members feel heard and validated. I share it with all my clients. Now I'm sharing it with you.

- Rule #1. Don't cancel or move meetings on short notice. Keep a consistent cadence people can count on. If you don't see value in the meetings, then your people won't either. If you prioritize other things over the meeting, then your people will, too.
- Rule #2. Don't break Rule #1.
- Rule #3. Don't say much. If you are talking more than 30% of the time in your team meetings, then that is an issue. I still struggle with this one, but I'm working on it.
- Rule #4. Make sure other people own portions of the agenda. This will promote a roundtable feel and empower your people.
- Rule #5. Don't do a mash-up of forecasting calls and weekly team meetings. That is like mixing oil and water. They simply don't work well inside the same window.
- Rule #6. Make sure the meeting preparation and outcomes are documented and discussed to have a smooth transition from one meeting to the next. The team meeting structure should feel like a journey, not a bunch of standalone events.
- Rule #7: Don't critique people in front of their peers. Save that for one-on-one coaching sessions.

Chapter Takeaways

- When leaders listen, cool things happen.
- Be present. Turn off phone notifications when you have meetings or one-on-ones. Don't have multiple screens open. Stop scrolling when you should be listening.
- Run effective sales meetings in which team members feel heard and validated.

EPILOGUE

The Power of "If"

Here is the final insight I want to share with you. In my opinion, the word "if" is the sales leader's secret weapon. It's the most powerful word there is when it comes to determining both mindset and possibility. Do you have a growth mindset or a static mindset? Do you see a future full of possibility or fraught with limitations? "If" will let you know in a heartbeat.

Start any sentence with the word "if," and see what you come up with. (Go ahead. Think of one right now.)

147

Whenever you start a sentence with "if," the sentence typically finishes with an intended or unintended outcome or consequence. That outcome or consequence tells you a lot about your current state of mind.

- If I go to the store, I will buy something I like.
- If I go to the store, I will waste money.
- If I go to the store, I'll probably wander around because I never know what to get.
- If I go to the store, I'll get something really good for dinner.
- If I get that manager job, I think half the team will leave.
- If I get that manager job, I'll probably mess up so bad I'll have to quit.
- If I get that manager job, I'll learn, grow, and help my team succeed.
- If I get that manager job, it'll be a huge positive step in my career.
- If I make a mistake, I'll never be able to recover.
- If I make a mistake, I'll use it as an experience to get better.

There are two key lessons to this exercise.

1. If you aren't creating "if" statements, you'll get stuck. You'll continue to repeat what you did yesterday.

2. You have 100% control over how you create the second half of the "if" sentence. You can limit progress with a negative mindset, or you can create new experiences through a shining lens about what is positive.

How about this:

▪ If I commit to asking myself "what if," then I will continue to challenge myself to change and grow.

If you have a growth mindset, you'll love "if." If you have a static mindset, you'll despise "if." Either way, it's your choice to decide which mindset you'll foster. Use "if" as a tool to clarify your attitudes towards future outcomes.

One of the paramount functions for any leader is to constantly challenge the current state. Use "if" statements to help challenge the status quo. Use "if" statements to clarify your own desired outcomes. Then share this powerful tool with those who look to you for leadership.

Here's my final challenge for you: Keep coming back to "if." Be intentional. Be present. Be positive. Be forward-focused. Make that your way of life and find a way to incorporate those mindsets into your management style, and you'll continue to emerge on purpose. You will make the climb. And you will reach the summit.

Look for these other books on shop.sandler.com:

SALES SERIES

The Art and Skill of Sales Psychology
Asking Questions the Sandler Way
Bootstrap Selling the Sandler Way
Call Center Success the Sandler Way
Digital Prospecting
The Contrarian Salesperson
LinkedIn the Sandler Way
Prospect the Sandler Way
Retail Success in an Online World
Sandler Enterprise Selling
The Sandler Rules
The Unapologetic Saleswoman
Why People Buy
You Can't Teach a Kid to Ride a Bike at a Seminar

MANAGEMENT & LEADERSHIP SERIES

Change the Sandler Way
Customer Service the Sandler Way
Lead When You Dance
Motivational Management the Sandler Way
Misery to Mastery
The Intentional Sales Manager
Th Right Hire
The Road to Excellence
The Sales Coach's Playbook
The Sandler Rules for Sales Leaders
The Success Cadence
Transforming Leaders the Sandler Way
Winning from Failing
21ˢᵗ Century Ride Along
Scaling Sales Success

PROFESSIONAL DEVELOPMENT SERIES

Accountability the Sandler Way
From the Board Room to the Living Room
Sandler Success Principles
Succeed the Sandler Way
Negotiating From the Inside Out

INDUSTRY SERIES

Making Channel Sales Work
Patient Care the Sandler Way
Selling in Manufacturing and Logistics
Selling Professional Services the Sandler Way
Selling to Homeowners the Sandler Way
Selling Technology the Sandler Way